Organizing for Learning

Organizing
for Learning

Strategies for
Knowledge Creation
and Enduring Change

by Daniel H. Kim

PEGASUS COMMUNICATIONS, INC.
WALTHAM

Library of Congress Cataloging-in-Publication Data

Kim, Daniel H., 1960 -
  Organizing for learning : strategies for knowledge creation and enduring change / by Daniel H. Kim.
    p. cm.
  Includes bibliographical references.
  ISBN 1-883823-54-4
  1. Organizational learning. I. Title.

  HD58.82.K56 2001
  658.4'038—dc21

                                                                    00-052878

Acquiring editor: Kellie Wardman O'Reilly
Editorial assistance provided by: Lauren Keller Johnson
Cover design: Fineline Communications
Interior design: Thompson-Steele Production Services
Production: Julie Quinn

Pegasus Communications, Inc. is dedicated to providing resources that help people explore, understand, articulate, and address the challenges they face in managing the complexities of a changing world. Since 1989, Pegasus has worked to build a community of organizational development practitioners through newsletters, books, audio and video tapes, and its annual *Systems Thinking in Action*® Conference and other events. For additional copies or information on volume discounts, contact:

PEGASUS COMMUNICATIONS, INC. • www.pegasuscom.com

PEGASUS
COMMUNICATIONS

Orders and Payments Offices:
P.O. Box 2241
Williston, VT 05495
Phone: (800) 272-0945 / (802) 862-0095
Fax: (802) 864-7626

Editorial and Business Offices:
One Moody Street
Waltham, MA 02453-5339
Phone: (781) 398-9700
Fax: (781) 894-7175

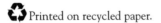 Printed on recycled paper.

05   04   03   02   01   8   7   6   5   4   3   2   1

5379

Acknowledgments

The work contained in this book builds on the prior work of many individuals, including Jay Forrester, founder of the field of system dynamics; W. Edwards Deming, statistician and quality pioneer; Peter Senge, author of *The Fifth Discipline*; and many other leaders and practitioners who are developing systems thinking ideas and concepts into a growing body of theory and practice. The chapters in this anthology originally appeared in *The Systems Thinker* Newsletter, and were edited by Kellie Wardman O'Reilly, Janice Molloy, Lauren Keller Johnson, and Colleen P. Lannon.

HOW TO READ CAUSAL LOOP DIAGRAMS

As you read the chapters in this book, you'll notice that many of them contain diagrams featuring circular arrows and labels such as "R," "s," and so forth. These *causal loop diagrams* consist of variables connected by arrows that show the movement of feedback through the system. Each arrow is labeled with a sign ("s" or "o") that indicates how one variable influences another. Here's an example of a simple CLD:

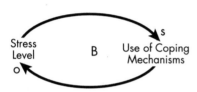

In this diagram, stress level and use of coping mechanisms are the two variables connected by feedback arrows. The "s" on the upper arrow means that when the stress level changes, the use of coping mechanisms changes in the *same* direction. For example, if the stress level increases, the use of coping mechanisms also increases. The "o" on the lower arrow means that when use of coping mechanisms changes, then the level of stress changes in the *opposite* direction. For instance, as use of coping mechanisms increases, the stress level decreases.

Causal loop diagrams are made up of a combination of balancing and reinforcing loops. The CLD we just "walked through" is an example of a balancing loop, as indicated by the "B" in the center. A balancing process tends to keep the system behavior relatively steady overall. In our example, for instance, the two variables balance each other and keep each other under control.

A reinforcing process, by contrast, drives change in one direction with even more change. Reinforcing processes are recognizable by the uncontrolled or exponential changes that they create. The figure below, labeled "R," is a simple example of this kind of dynamic.

In this reinforcing loop, each arrow is labeled with an "s" for same direction of change. To read this diagram, you would say that "as marketing increases, so do sales, which leads to more funds available for marketing, which leads to even more marketing."

Balancing and reinforcing processes occur in infinite combinations in the systems we see all around us, including behavior within organizations.

Contents

Introduction

As the rules of competition change at an increasing pace, the very foundations on which business has rested for so long are shifting. New technologies such as the Web are transforming the way firms do business, the forces of globalization continue to change the very definition of markets, and knowledge has superseded capital as the core asset of any company.

In the face of such challenges, the current buzz in management circles deals with the topic of knowledge management. This current focus on managing knowledge is fueled in part by the relentless pace of technological progress and the rapid speed at which innovations in one part of the world spread to the rest of the globe in an ever shrinking marketplace. The irony is that many organizations are fixated on the *management* of knowledge rather than its *creation* even as the rapid pace of change is making existing knowledge obsolete at an ever increasing rate.

Knowledge Warehouses vs. Knowledge Generators

When people talk about knowledge management, they tend to assume as a given that useful knowledge is and will continue to be generated, and that the task at hand is to figure out better ways to "manage" that cornucopia of knowledge. What is typically meant by "managing knowledge" is figuring out how to store, retrieve, and leverage the knowledge that is available, both inside and outside one's organization. It is not surprising, then, that many efforts tend to focus on designing and managing better knowledge "warehouses" rather than on understanding and developing better knowledge "generators."

In a warehouse view of the world, we try to design the most efficient and cost-effective system for the storage and retrieval of the knowledge (which is often synonymous with information) we possess in our organization. We pay attention to the parameters that are consistent with how we might design and manage a warehouse of physical inventory—the accounting of what stuff is there, how space-efficient we can be, how fast we can move the stuff around, how many people utilize it, what the carrying and usage costs are, etc.

From a systems thinking perspective, however, we want to shift our focus from managing existing knowledge to a focus on the creating of new knowledge. In essence, we are interested in understanding what it means to organize for learning, to focus on developing the knowledge-creation side of our work.

Organizing for Learning

The last decade has witnessed a remarkable ripening of the field of organizational learning—especially the discipline of systems thinking. Organizations large and small, well known and anonymous, have put the tools and principles of this field to work, with striking results. But as with any era marked by dramatic shifts in the way people live and work, the ride has not always been smooth. One challenge that continues to be difficult centers on a deceptively simple question: How can we best transfer individual learning to the organizational level?

Compounding the challenge of addressing this question is the breakdown of the old "contract" between companies and workers—in which people expected to work a lifetime for one employer. In its place is a new world of work in which people freely change jobs *and* employers, on the assumption that it's up to them to develop their own skills and experience so as to remain as employable as possible. Although this kind of shift may lead to greater flexibility and increased capability, the downside is that when workers leave a position or a company, they take important knowledge and learning with them.

All this points even more to the need for organizations to understand the true nature of company-level learning and to put the systems, structures, and strategies in place that will let it flourish. Instead of taking organizational learning for granted, we need to pay attention to the ways in which we organize for or against effective learning and enhanced knowledge creation.

To this end, *Organizing for Learning: Strategies for Knowledge Creation and Enduring Change*, a collection of lead articles from THE SYSTEMS THINKER Newsletter, offers an array of ideas that will stimulate your thinking about how you can help your own organizations become better organized for learning. Addressed to executives and front-line managers alike, the book is organized around three major themes:

- Part One, **Organizational Learning and Knowledge Creation,** provides a broader perspective of the knowledge-creation process. It focuses especially on the interplay among theories, methods and tools, and practical knowledge—all in the context of a learning community. You will also find a framework for understanding how individual learning translates into organizational learning as a cyclical phenomenon, and ideas for developing and leveraging organizational competence.

- Part Two, **The Power of Theory,** argues for a new role for managers: that of theory-builders. Academic theorizing is not the focus here. Instead, this kind of process takes center stage in organizations that are interested in maximizing learning—because only through developing and testing explicit theories about our organization and our business are we capable of learning. Without theory, we learn from neither our failures nor our successes.

- Part Three, **A Systemic Approach to Creating Enduring Change,** offers a systemic framework for managing large-scale change efforts. The Vision Deployment Matrix, the Levels of Perspective, and the concept of Action Modes provide a systemic method and a set of tools to help managers test their own theories about change as they work to improve their organization's performance.

No Theory, No Learning

Dr. Deming, statistician and quality pioneer, once said, "No theory, no learning." That is the central message of this book tying the three parts firmly together. Our mental models—our theories about how the world works—arguably constitute the most important force shaping the fate of our organizations. As this book maintains, only by articulating, testing, and, if necessary, changing our mental models can we create a work culture in which learning can thrive. This requires that we not only think differently, but also frame problems in whole new ways, a capacity that is essential for those who are interested in being in the knowledge-creation business.

Part One

Organizational Learning and Knowledge Creation

One of the main features of the current Industrial Age thinking is reductionistic thinking—the belief that we can understand complex things by breaking them down into smaller and smaller parts. The power of this thinking is demonstrated through the process of analysis, which has proven to be highly useful in advancing our understanding of many complex systems. It has worked so well that we have shifted the primary focus of our attention to the pieces of a system rather than the system as a whole, and worse, have even worked on the pieces without really taking into account the context of the larger system of which they are a part.

Any encounter with the traditional healthcare system in the U.S. quickly demonstrates how much we have embraced this reductionistic approach. We are sent to specialists who are highly knowledgeable about a specific human body part, and they usually treat that part as if it were a disembodied thing unto itself. Organizations also approach their ills in the same way, focusing on problem areas with the assumption that they can be fixed by working on that specific area, as if the areas were separate from the rest of the organization.

When systems are loosely coupled (i.e., the parts do not require close coordination within a short period of time), this focus on analyzing parts may not pose too many problems (that we can see!). However, as the speed of change increases, it often increases the interdependencies within the system as changes in one part of the system have more immediate impact on other parts. This is true at both the micro and macro levels of any system.

We begin this section by looking at creating knowledge in the larger macro system we call our society or community. In our article, **"From Fragmentation to Integration: Building Learning Communities"** (p. 9), Peter Senge and I take a systemic look at the way in which humans create knowledge and why the current fragmented approach may not be getting us the results we want. We identify three core functions—research, capacity-building, and practice—which need to be integrated in order for us to learn effectively as a community of people regardless of scale. In other words, the interdependent integration of these three functions is important whether we are talking about a small project-team trying to improve a production process, an organization trying to reinvent itself, a nation wanting to become more competitive in the global marketplace, or a species trying to understand how to live on this planet in a more sustainable way.

Of course, knowledge creation implies learning, and in the context of social institutions, it requires organizational learning. Although people talk a lot about organizational learning as if it were happening all the time, it is not always clear what is meant by organizational learning or how it is different from individual learning. Yet, if we are really interested in understanding and managing the knowledge-creation process, we need a way to see and talk about the link between individual learning and organizational learning. In **"Managing Organizational Learning Cycles"** (p. 19), I offer a model for conceptualizing how individual learning is integrated with organizational learning so that we can take a more active role in supporting the kinds of learning that will contribute to the organization's success. (For a longer version of this article, please see "The Link between Individual and Organizational Learning," The Sloan Management Review, Vol 35, No. 1.) In particular, we explore several learning "disconnects" which can either degrade or enhance learning (situational, fragmented, and opportunistic learning) depending on the circumstances.

The last article in this section focuses on the challenge of persisting in one's investments in organizational learning in order to be able to generate new knowledge. All too often, organizations catch the latest management buzz and pour a lot of time and money into learning about some new tools and concepts. But, without a sufficiently deep understanding of those new approaches, there *are often few tangible results to show for the investments, and so they abandon those efforts as quickly as they jumped on them. In **"Leveraging Competence to Build Organizational Capability"** (p. 29), I share a five-stage model of skill acquisition that lays out the progressive stages that must be developed if you are truly interested in attaining a level of competence in new knowledge creation (vs. old knowledge regurgitation). Most organizations do not stick with a new area long enough to get people to the stage of "Competent," which is the minimal level of capability required to become your own knowledge generators. Thus, most organizations are not able to benefit from the potential of many good ideas because they lack the discipline of sticking with it. My hope is that this model provides a roadmap for understanding what and how long it takes to build a critical threshold of competence.*

Chapter One

From Fragmentation to Integration: Building Learning Communities

by Peter M. Senge and Daniel H. Kim

"We live in an era of massive institutional failure," says Dee Hock, founder and CEO emeritus of Visa International. We need only look around us to see evidence to support Dee's statement. Corporations, for example, are spending millions of dollars to teach high-school graduates in their workforces to read, write, and perform basic arithmetic. Our healthcare system is in a state of acute crisis. The U.S. spends more on healthcare than any other industrialized country, and yet the health of our citizens is the worst among those same nations. Our educational system is increasingly coming under fire for not preparing our children adequately to meet the demands of the future. Our universities are losing credibility. Our religious institutions are struggling to maintain relevance in people's lives. Our government is increasingly dysfunctional, caught in a vicious cycle of growing special-interest groups, distrust, and corruption. The corporation may be the healthiest institution in the U.S. today, which isn't saying much.

One of the reasons for this widespread institutional failure is that the *knowledge-creating system*, the method by which human beings collectively learn and by which society's institutions improve and revitalize them-

9

selves, is deeply fragmented. This fragmentation has developed so gradually that few of us have noticed it; we take the disconnections between the branches of knowledge and between knowledge and practice as a given.

A Knowledge-Creating System

Before we can address the issue of fragmentation, we need to establish what has been fragmented. In other words, what do we mean by a knowledge-creating system, and what does it mean to say it is fragmented?

We believe that human communities have always attempted to organize themselves to maximize the production, transmittal, and application of knowledge. In these activities, different individuals fulfill different roles, with varying degrees of success. For example, in indigenous cultures, elders articulate timeless principles grounded in their experience to guide their tribes' future actions. "Doers," whether warriors, growers, hunters, or nannies, try to learn how to do things better than before and continually improve their craft. And coaches and teachers help people develop their capacities to both perform their roles and grow as human beings. These three activities—which we can term theory-building, practice, and capacity-building—are intertwined and woven into the fabric of the community in a seamless process that restores and advances the knowledge of the tribe. One could argue that this interdependent knowledge-creating system is the only way that human beings collectively learn, generate new knowledge, and change their world.

We can view this system for producing knowledge as a cycle. People apply available knowledge to accomplish their goals. This practical application in turn provides experiential data from which new theories can be formulated to guide future action. New theories and principles then lead to new methods and tools that translate theory into practical know-how, the pursuit of new goals, and new experience—and the cycle continues.

Imagine that this cycle of knowledge creation is a tree (see "The Cycle of Knowledge-Creation"). The tree's roots are the theories. Like theories, the roots are invisible to most of the world, and yet the health of the root system to a large extent determines the health of the tree. The branches are the methods and tools, which enable translation of theories into new

THE CYCLE OF KNOWLEDGE CREATION

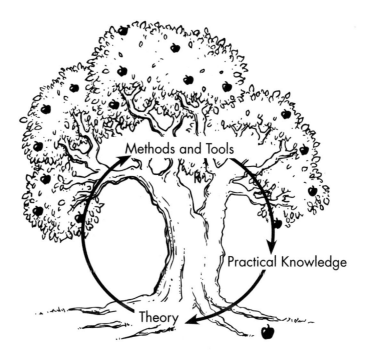

Methods and Tools

Practical Knowledge

Theory

Like theories, the tree's roots are invisible, and yet the health of the root system determines the health of the tree. The branches are the methods and tools, which enable translation of theories into new capabilities and practical results. The fruit is that practical knowledge. The tree as a whole is a system.

capabilities and practical results. The fruit is that practical knowledge. In a way, the whole system seems designed to produce the fruit. But, if you harvest and eat *all* the fruit from the tree, eventually there will be no more trees. So, some of the fruit must be used to provide the seeds for more trees. The tree as a whole is a system.

The tree is a wonderful metaphor, because it functions through a profound, amazing transformational process called photosynthesis. The roots absorb nutrients from the soil. Eventually, the nutrients flow through the trunk and into the branches and leaves. In the leaves, the nutrients interact with sunlight to create complex carbohydrates, which serve as the basis for development of the fruit.

So, what are the metaphorical equivalents that allow us to create fruits of practical knowledge in our organizations? We can view research activities as expanding the root system to build better and richer theories. Capacity-building activities extend the branches by translating the theories into usable methods and tools. The use of these methods and tools enhances people's capabilities. The art of practice in a particular line of work transforms the theories, methods, and tools into usable knowledge as people apply their capabilities to practical tasks, much as the process of photosynthesis converts the nutrients into leaves, flowers, and fruit. In our society,

- **Research** represents any disciplined approach to discovery and understanding with a commitment to share what's being learned. We're not referring to white-coated scientists performing laboratory experiments; we mean research in the same way that a child asks, "What's going on here?" By pursuing such questions, research—whether performed by academics or thoughtful managers or consultants reflecting on their experiences—continually generates new theories about how our world works.

- **Practice** is anything that a group of people does to produce a result. It's the application of energy, tools, and effort to achieve something practical. An example is a product-development team that wants to build a better product more quickly at a lower cost. By directly applying the available theory, tools, and methods in our work, we generate practical knowledge.

- **Capacity-building** links research and practice. It is equally committed to discovery and understanding and to practical know-how and results. Every learning community includes coaches, mentors, and teachers—people who help others build skills and capabilities through developing new methods and tools that help make theories practical.

"The Stocks and Flows of Knowledge Creation" shows how the various elements are linked together in a knowledge-creating system.

Institutionalized Fragmentation

If knowledge is best created by this type of integrated system, how did our current systems and institutions become so fragmented? To answer that question, we need to look at how research, practice, and capacity-building are institutionalized in our culture (see "The Fragmentation of Institutions," p. 14).

For example, what institution do we most associate with research? Universities. What does the world of practice encompass? Corporations,

THE STOCKS AND FLOWS OF KNOWLEDGE CREATION

Research activities build better and richer theories. Capacity-building functions translate the theories into usable methods and tools. The use of these methods and tools enhances people's capabilities. The art of practice transforms the theories, methods, and tools into practical knowledge, as people apply their capabilities to practical tasks.

schools, hospitals, and nonprofits. And what institution do we most associate with capacity-building—people helping people in the practical world? Consulting, or the HR function within an organization. Each of these institutions has made that particular activity its defining core. And, because research, practice, and capacity-building each operate within the walls of separate institutions, it is easy for the people within these institutions to feel cut off from each other, leading to suspicion, stereotyping, and an "us" versus "them" mindset.

Technical Rationality: One Root of Fragmentation

How did we reach this state of fragmentation? Over hundreds of years, we have developed a notion that knowledge is the province of the expert, the researcher, the academic. Often, the very term *science* is used to connote this kind of knowledge, as if the words that come out of the mouths of scientists are somehow inherently more truthful than everyone else's words.

THE FRAGMENTATION OF INSTITUTIONS

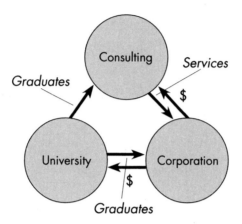

Because research, practice, and capacity-building each operate within the walls of separate institutions, the people within these institutions feel cut off from each other, leading to suspicion, stereotyping, and an "us" versus "them" mindset.

Donald Schön has called this concept of knowledge "technical rationality." First you develop the theory, then you apply it. Or, first the experts come in and figure out what's wrong, and then you use their advice to fix the problem. Of course, although the advice may be brilliant, sometimes we just can't figure out how to implement it.

But maybe the problem isn't in the advice. Maybe it's in the basic assumption that this method is how learning or knowledge creation actually works. Maybe the problem is really in this very way of thinking: that first you must get "the answer," then you must apply it.

The implicit notion of technical rationality often leads to conflict between executives and the front-line people in organizations. Executives often operate by the notion of technical rationality: In Western culture, being a boss means having all the answers. However, front-line people know much more than they can ever say about their jobs and about the organization. They actually have the capability to *do* something, not just *talk* about something. Technical rationality is great if all you ever have to do is talk.

Organizing for Learning

If we let go of this notion of technical rationality, we can then start asking more valuable questions, such as:

- How does real learning occur?
- How do new capabilities develop?
- How do learning communities that interconnect theory and practice, concept and capability come into being?
- How do they sustain themselves and grow?
- What forces can destroy them, undermine them, or cause them to wither?

Clearly, we need a theory, method, and set of tools for organizing the learning efforts of groups of people.

Real learning is often far more complex—and more interesting—than the theory of technical rationality suggests. We often develop significant new capabilities with only an incomplete idea of *how we do what we do*. As in skiing or learning to ride a bicycle, we "do it" before we really understand the actual concept. Similarly, practical know-how often precedes new principles and general methods in organizational learning. Yet, this pattern of learning can also be problematic.

For example, teams within a large institution can produce significant innovations, but this new knowledge often fails to spread. Modest improvements may spread quickly, but real breakthroughs are difficult to diffuse. Brilliant innovations won't spread if there is no way for them to spread; in other words, if there is no way for an organization to extract the general lessons from such innovations and develop new methods and tools for sharing those lessons. The problem is that wide diffusion of learning requires the same commitment to research and capacity-building as it does to practical results. Yet few businesses foster such commitment. Put differently, organizational learning requires a *community* that enhances research, capacity-building, and practice.

Learning Communities

We believe that the absence of effective learning communities limits our ability to learn from each other, from what goes on within the organization, and from our most clearly demonstrated breakthroughs. Imagine a learning community as a group of people that bridges the worlds of research, practice, and capacity-building to produce the kind of knowledge that has the power to transform the way we operate, not merely make incremental improvements. If we are interested in innovation and in the vitality of large institutions, then we are interested in creating learning communities that *integrate* knowledge instead of fragment it.

In a learning community, people view each of the three functions—research, capacity-building, practice—as vital to the whole (see "A Learning Community"). Practice is crucial because it produces tangible results that show that the community has learned something. Capacity-building is important because it makes improvement possible. Research is also key because it provides a way to share learning with people in other parts of the organization and with future generations within the organization. In a learning community, people assume responsibility for the knowledge-creating process.

Learning Communities in Action

To commit to this knowledge-creating process, we must first understand what a learning community looks like in action in our organizations. Imagine a typical change initiative in an organization; for example, a product-development team trying a new approach to the way it handles engineering changes. Traditionally, such a team would be primarily interested in improving the results on its own projects. Team members probably wouldn't pay as much attention to deepening their understanding of why a new approach works better, or to creating new methods and tools for others to use. Nor would they necessarily attempt to share their learnings as widely as possible—they might well see disseminating the information as someone else's responsibility.

In a learning community, however, from the outset, the team conceives of the initiative as a way to maximize learning for itself *as well as* for other teams in the organization. Those involved in the research process are integral members of the team, not outsiders who poke at the system from a disconnected and fragmented perspective. The knowledge-creating process functions in real time within the organization, in a seamless cycle of practice, research, and capacity-building.

A LEARNING COMMUNITY

In a learning community, people view each of the three functions—research, capacity-building, practice—as vital to the whole.[1]

[1]The origins of this diagram unfolded as follows: The MIT Organizational Learning Center (OLC) Design Team first depicted the research, practice, and capacity-building activities as three interlocked circles in its thinking about learning communities. The diagram took its final form when John Shibley drew it as three interweaving "spheres of influence" during a meeting of the "Animators Group" at the OLC. The Three Spiral Diagram has since become a central metaphor for learning communities.

Imagine if this were the way in which we approached learning and change in all of our major institutions. What impact might this approach have on the health of any of our institutions, and on society as a whole? Given the problems we face within our organizations and within the larger culture, do we *have* any choice but to seek new ways to work together to face the challenges of the future? We believe the time has come for us to begin the journey back from fragmentation to wholeness and integration. The time has come for true learning communities to emerge. ⪌

Peter M. Senge is a senior lecturer at the Massachusetts Institute of Technology, where he is part of the Organizational Learning and Change group. He is also chairman of the Society for Organizational Learning (SoL). He is the author of the widely acclaimed book *The Fifth Discipline: The Art and Practice of the Learning Organization*, and, with colleagues (Charlotte Roberts, Rick Ross, Bryan Smith, and Art Kleiner), coauthor of *The Fifth Discipline Fieldbook: Strategies and Tools for Building a Learning Organization*, *The Dance of Change*, and *Schools That Learn*.

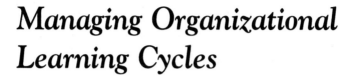

Chapter Two

Managing Organizational Learning Cycles

I magine an organization in which all the records disintegrated overnight. Suddenly, there are no more reports, no computer files, no employee records, no operating manuals, no calendars—all that remain are the people, buildings, capital equipment, raw materials, and inventory. Now imagine an organization where all of the people have mysteriously disappeared. The organization is left intact in every other way, but there are no employees. Which organization will find it easier to rebuild its former status, to continue to take actions, and to learn?

One may be tempted to conclude that substituting new people would be easier than replacing all the information and systems. But even in the most bureaucratic organization, with all its standard operating procedures and established protocols, there is much more about the firm that is unsaid and unwritten. In fact, numerical and verbal databases capture only a small fraction of the information that is in mental "databases."

The essence of an organization is embodied in its people, not its systems. The intangible assets of a company reside in the individual mental models that contribute to the organization's memory. Without these mental models—which include the subtle interconnections that have been developed among the members—an organization will be incapacitated in both learning and action. Yet in most organizations, individual mental databases are not "backed up," nor is the transfer from individual to organizational learning well managed. A critical challenge for a learning organization is understanding the transfer process through which individual

INDIVIDUAL LEARNING CYCLE

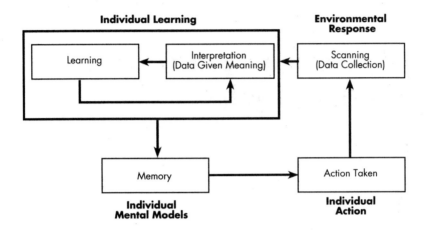

Learning at the individual level can be described as a cycle in which the person assimilates new data, reflects on past experiences, draws a conclusion, and then acts.

Adapted from Daft and Weick (1984).

learning and knowledge (mental models) become embedded in an organization's memory and structure. Once we have a clear understanding of this transfer process, we can actively manage organizational learning to be consistent with an organization's goals, vision, and values.

From Individual Learning . . .

In order to develop a framework for organizational learning, we must begin by understanding how individuals learn. The "Individual Learning Cycle" diagram shows a simplified model of individual learning. The diagram traces the process through which the brain assimilates some new data (environmental response), takes into account the memories of past experiences, comes to some conclusion about the new piece of information (individual learning), and then stores it away (individual mental models). After processing the new learning, one may choose to act or simply do nothing (individual action).

The processing stage has been labeled "individual mental models" because it represents much more than the traditional concept of memory.

Memory connotes a rather static repository for knowledge, whereas mental models involve the active creation of new knowledge. Mental models represent a person's view of the world, including both explicit and implicit understandings. They also provide the context in which to view and interpret new material, and they determine how stored information will be applied to a given situation.

. . . To Organizational Learning

In the early stages of an organization's existence, organizational learning is often synonymous with individual learning since it usually involves a very small group of people and the organization has minimal structure. As an organization grows, however, a distinction between the two levels of learning emerges. Somewhere in that process, a system evolves for capturing learnings from its individual members.

There is little agreement on what constitutes "appropriate" learning—those individual actions or learnings that should be transferred from the individual into the organization's memory. Standard operating procedures (SOPs), for example, are viewed as an important part of an organization's memory—a repository of past learning. But SOPs can also be a roadblock to learning if an organization becomes locked into old procedures and avoids searching for entirely new modes of behavior. How does an organization decide when once-appropriate routines are no longer valid? Can an organization anticipate obsolescence of its SOPs, or must it always learn by first making inappropriate decisions in the face of changing conditions? These are the kinds of issues a model of organizational learning must address.

Organizational Learning Cycles

By extending our model of individual learning to include organizational learning, we can begin to explore the transfer process between the two (see "A Simple Model of Organizational Learning" on p. 22). This model represents the organizational learning cycle as a four-stage process, with organizational learning composed of three distinct substages: individual learning, individual mental models, and organizational memory. Individual actions are taken based on individual mental models. These actions, in turn, translate into organizational action, and both actions

A SIMPLE MODEL OF ORGANIZATIONAL LEARNING

In this simple model of organizational learning, individual actions translate into organizational actions, producing some outcome (environmental response). The environmental response feeds back to affect individual learning, which in turn influences individual mental models and organizational memory.

produce some environmental response. The cycle is complete when the environmental response, in turn, leads to individual learning and affects individual mental models and organizational memory.

This simple model captures the transfer of individual learning to organizational memory via changes in individual mental models. Thus, organizational learning is separated from action (because not all learning translates into taking new actions) and from environmental response (because not all learning is precipitated by the environment). The complete learning cycle, however, does include both the actions of the individual and the organization as well as the environmental response to those actions.

An Integrated Model

There are at least two fundamentally different levels of learning at which an organization must be equally adept—operational and conceptual. *Operational learning* deals with the changes in the way we actually do things—filling out entry forms, operating a piece of machinery, handling a switchboard, retooling a machine, etc. While operational learning emphasizes the *how* of doing things, *conceptual learning* emphasizes the *why* of doing things—that is, it has do with the *thinking* behind why things are done in the first place. Conceptual learning deals with issues that challenge the very nature or existence of prevailing conditions or procedures. In order for organizational learning to be effective, however, conceptual learning must be operationalized into specific skills that can be learned and executed.

Individual Mental Models: Frameworks and Routines. Individual learning is captured in mental models through two different paths (see "Organizational Learning: An Integrated Model"). Operational learning produces new or revised routines that replace old or outworn ones. Conceptual learning leads to changes in frameworks, leading to new ways of looking at the world and new actions. For example, a design engineer may follow a six-step process for getting her drawings ready for a program

ORGANIZATIONAL LEARNING: AN INTEGRATED MODEL

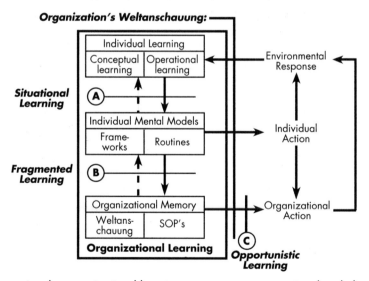

Improving the organizational learning process means managing the whole cycle—individual learning, organizational learning, and the links between the two. At the same time, barriers to organizational learning (A, B, and C) must be addressed.

review meeting. Through experience, she may learn to improve the process by streamlining some of the steps involved (operational learning). As she rethinks the *framework* of her work—the context in which the drawings are being produced and what their use is—she may question the production of the drawings themselves and identify situations when the drawings may not be necessary (conceptual learning). Her revised mental models will contain *both* the new frameworks and routines as well as the knowledge about how the routines fit within the new framework.

  Organizational Memory: Weltanschauung and SOPs. The dual pathway continues from mental models to organizational memory. Over time, individual mental frameworks become embedded into the organiza-tion's own *Weltanschauung,* or worldview. An organization's view of the world, in turn, affects how the individual interprets changes in the envi-ronment and how she translates her mental models into action. It also

====================

If an organization assumes that it can take an active role in affecting its environment, this organization may approach everything in the spirit of experimentation, testing, and inventing.

====================

influences how the organization translates its organizational memory into action. For example, if an organization believes that its ability to affect the environment is low, it will rely on standard routines and reactive behav-iors. If, on the other hand, an organization assumes that it can take an active role in affecting its environment, this organization may approach everything in the spirit of experimentation, testing, and inventing.

  In similar fashion, individual routines that have proven sound over time become a company's standard operating procedures. The strength of the link between individual mental models and organizational memory depends on how influential an individual or group is. In the case of a CEO or upper manager, influence can be high due to the power inherent in the positions. Similarly, a united group of hourly workers can have a high degree of influence owing to its size.

Incomplete Learning Cycles

Organizational learning requires completing the entire loop. If any of the links are either weak or broken, learning can be impaired. *Situational* learning, for example, occurs when the link between individual learning and individual mental models is severed: That is, the learning is situation-specific and does not change mental models. Crisis management is one example of situational learning in which each problem is solved but no learning is carried over to the next case.

When the link between individual models and organizational memory is broken, *fragmented* learning occurs. Individual mental models may change, but those changes are not reflected in the organization's memory. When organizational learning is fragmented among isolated individuals (or groups), the loss of the individuals (through turnover or layoffs) means loss of knowledge as well.

The link between organizational memory and organizational action, if broken, can lead to *opportunistic* learning. This occurs when organizational actions are pursued without taking into account organizational memory or the organization's values, culture, and SOPs. Sometimes this is done purposefully, when one wishes to bypass the features of an organization that may impede progress on a specific front. The use of "skunk works" to develop the IBM personal computer is a good example, as is General Motors' creation of an entirely new car division, Saturn.

Managing the Whole Learning Cycle

Managing organizational learning means managing the complete cycle—*explicitly*. Improving each of the pieces is not enough—the links between the pieces must also be managed. This requires addressing each of the incomplete learning cycles described above.

Beyond Situational Learning. Mental models are the critical pathways between individual learning and organizational memory. Mental models are the managers and arbiters of how new information will be acquired, retained, used, and deleted. Although a company can try to manage the flow of information, control the environment, or manipulate peoples' learning environment in various ways, if a person's view of the world remains unchanged, it is unlikely that any such actions will affect the quality of learning.

Therefore, closing the loop on situational learning—the link between individual learning and individual mental models—requires developing individuals' ability to transfer specific insights into more general maps that will guide them in the future. In order to make mental models explicit, we need appropriate tools to capture the type of knowledge that is being mapped.

Dynamic systems, in particular, require a different set of tools for making mental models explicit. Systems archetypes (systemic structures that recur repeatedly in diverse settings) such as "Shifting the Burden" and "Tragedy of the Commons" can be very helpful for eliciting and capturing managers' intuitive understanding of complex dynamic issues. *Action Maps* are also useful for capturing the behavioral dynamics of a team or organization over time. They help managers see the larger patterns of behavior in which their specific actions are embedded. Together, these two methods can help surface and capture a great deal of tacit individual knowledge in a way in which it can be shared, challenged, and subject to change—thus transferring it to organizational memory.

From Fragmented to Organizational Learning. Capturing individual mental models alone is not sufficient to achieve organizational learning, however. There also needs to be a way to prevent fragmented learning among individuals and to spread the learning throughout the organization. One way to accomplish this is through the design and implementation of *learning laboratories*—managerial practice fields where teams of managers can practice and learn together.

Learning laboratories can be designed, in part, around the learnings captured in systems archetypes and Action Maps. The spirit of the learning lab is one of active experimentation and inquiry, where everyone participates in surfacing and testing each other's mental models. Through this process, a shared understanding of the key assumptions and interrelationships of the organization can emerge. The use of an interactive computer management flight simulator offers the participants an opportunity to test their assumptions and to viscerally experience the consequences of their actions. The learning laboratory can be the vehicle through which organizational memory—via its *Weltanschauung* and SOPs—can be enriched over time.

Harnessing Opportunistic Learning. If the organization's own culture and ways of doing things get in the way of learning, scenario planning and idealized designs can provide a way to break out of the norms. Royal Dutch/Shell used scenario planning to create alternative realities that stretched beyond what most managers in the company could envision. By carefully constructing a multiple set of possible scenarios, Shell was successful in anticipating and adapting to extremely volatile environments.

Idealized designs, used by Russell Ackoff and his colleagues at Interact (Bala Cynwyd, PA), can also minimize the amount of influence an organization's current state has in determining its future. The principal idea is to start by crystallizing an ideal future without considering the current capabilities or organizational limitations. Thus, the planning process is "pulled" by where you want to be instead of "anchored" by where you are.

The Learning Challenge

The old model of a hierarchical corporation where the top thinks and the bottom acts is giving way to a new model where thinking and acting must occur at all levels. As organizations push for flatter structures and reduced bureaucracy, there will be increased reliance on the individuals to be the carriers of the organization's knowledge. Instead of codifying rules and procedures in handbooks and policy manuals, the new challenge is to continually capture the emerging understanding of the organization wherever it unfolds. At the heart of it all is understanding the role that individual mental models play in the organizational learning cycle and continually finding ways to manage the transfer from individual to organizational learning. ⌖

Chapter Three

Leveraging Competence to Build Organizational Capability

"If calculus were invented today, our organizations would not be able to learn it. We'd send everyone off to a three-day intensive program. We'd then tell everyone to try to apply what they'd learned. After three to six months we'd assess whether it was working. We'd undoubtedly then conclude that this 'calculus stuff' wasn't all it was made out to be and go off and look for something else to improve results." (Peter Senge et al., *The Fifth Discipline Fieldbook*).

As the quote above illustrates, in today's fast-paced business world, we seldom have the appropriate time perspective when investing in the acquisition of new skills. We tend to want things to be available in bite-sized chunks that we can conveniently fit into our busy schedules, and we want to see immediate results from those investments. Sending people to short skill-building workshops may be adequate for adding to a base of knowledge they already possess, such as training on a new machine or with a new accounting-software package. If, on the other hand, we are interested in developing capabilities that are quite different from our current base of experience and skill, this approach is likely to produce disappointing results.

Developing Organizational Learning Capabilities

For many organizations, developing the capabilities to support organizational learning requires the acquisition of markedly different skills from those they are currently using. In the absence of a solid understanding of what it really takes to develop such skills, many organizations fall into the trap described in the opening quote and abandon their efforts prematurely. The challenge multiplies when the skills involved function as an ensemble whose interdependent development is more important than the development of each one separately.

In *The Fifth Discipline*, Peter Senge defines learning organizations as those that continually enhance their capacity to create the results they truly care about. In our work at the Society for Organizational Learning (formerly the MIT Organizational Learning Center), we often talk about investing in three core capabilities to support organizational learning. We use the analogy of a three-legged stool to represent the interdependence of those three capabilities (see "Three-Legged Stool").

The Aspiration leg of the stool focuses on developing a clear sense of purpose and vision both at the individual and at the larger organizational levels (disciplines of Personal Mastery and Shared Vision). The

---

THREE-LEGGED STOOL

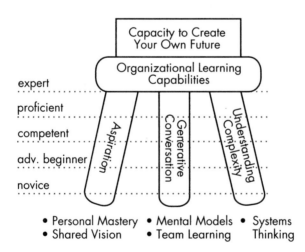

The stool represents the interdependence of three core capabilities to support organizational learning: Aspiration, Generative Conversation, and Understanding Complexity. Together, these three capabilities allow us to create our future.

Source: Society for Organizational Learning

Generative Conversation leg centers on expanding our capacity to be more reflective in our thinking and to become more generative when we think and talk with others (disciplines of Mental Models and Team Learning). Understanding Complexity emphasizes internalizing perspectives and skills, which allows us to better understand and manage systemic interconnections that produce complex organizational dynamics (discipline of Systems Thinking). Together, these three capabilities allow us to create our future. They enable us to articulate clear visions of what results we want; they give us the capacity to have productive conversations about how to make those results happen; and they provide us with the conceptual tools and thinking to manage the complexities involved.

The image of the stool conveys a couple of important points. First, the stool must have all three legs to be stable enough to support anything, especially the capacity to create your own future. Second, if you do not develop these capabilities more or less together as an ensemble, the stool will have legs of different lengths and will be too wobbly to support anything for very long. So, even though you might experience momentary success in creating your own future, it will be short-lived if you do not balance the development of the three core capabilities.

A relevant question at this point might be, "How do we know the length of each leg at any point in time?" In other words, what kind of common measurement can we use to gauge how we are doing over time, across a diverse set of capabilities? To answer these questions, we need a framework for talking together about what it means to develop each of these capabilities.

A Five-Stage Model of Skill Acquisition

Dreyfus and Dreyfus, in their book *Mind Over Machines*, offer a five-stage model of skill acquisition that provides a useful starting point in answering the questions posed above. They start by making a distinction between "knowing that" (knowing that certain rules and principles apply in a given situation) versus "knowing how" (being able to actually use the particular skill). These two kinds of knowledge are not equal, and having one doesn't necessarily mean you have the other.

For example, although you obviously possess an expert's know-how about walking, you probably can't translate that capability into rules and procedures that would allow someone else to replicate the skill. In other words, you possess the "know-how" for walking but you don't necessarily "know that" certain principles and movements allow you to produce that action; you just do it. In other situations where you might be a novice, like downhill skiing, you may clearly understand that you are supposed to keep your skis parallel, lean forward, and allow your legs to work like shock absorbers, but you may not be able to convert that knowledge into know-how that lets you ski gracefully down the slopes. As you struggle to keep your skis from crossing and end up tumbling down the slope, you are demonstrating the gap between "knowing that" and "knowing how."

Based on extensive studies, Dreyfus and Dreyfus conclude that people generally go through five distinct stages from rule-guided "knowing that" to experienced-based "knowing how." These stages are: Novice, Advanced Beginner, Competent, Proficient, and Expert. Each stage reflects different levels of competence in a number of specific capabilities, such as overall perception of a task situation and ability to exercise judgment (see "Five Stages of Skill Acquisition").

Novice. At this stage, learners have a beginning awareness of the existence of a particular subject area, but only at the level of abstract concepts and ideas. The instructor must clearly and objectively define elements of the situation to be treated so the novice can recognize them without reference to the overall situation in which they occur. Novices possess little or no ability to put ideas into practice in a reliable way. They apply their nascent skills by following a set of rules without regard for the context in which they are operating.

Advanced Beginner. Performance improves to a marginally acceptable level only after novices have considerable experience coping in real settings. Through repeated exposure to many situations, advanced beginners gain a deeper appreciation of the subject area and acknowledge their own lack of knowledge about the discipline as a whole. At the same time, they learn to apply principles and tools in contexts that are similar to well-defined cases they have studied. That is, advanced beginners can reliably follow the prescribed steps of a process, provided the situation closely matches ones they have previously encountered.

Competent. Achieving competence means having had exposure to, and a working familiarity with, the full array of knowledge that comprises the particular subject. At this stage, learners have received all the "knowing that" there is to know—additional instructions and tips will not

FIVE STAGES OF SKILL ACQUISITION

	Novice	Advanced Beginner	Competent	Proficient	Expert
Processing of Elements of a Situation	Sees only those that are clearly and objectively defined	Perceives similarity with prior examples	Reflects upon various alternatives to goal	Intuitively organizes and understands task without decomposing it into component features	Intuitively organizes and understands task without decomposing it into component features
Rules of Behavior/ Decision- Making	Follows "context-free" rules	Applies situation matching	Analytically calculates choices that best achieve goal	Consciously focuses on choice that best achieves intuitive plan	Acts in an unconscious, automatic, and natural way
Exercising of Judgment	None	None	Consciously deliberates	Acts based on prior concrete examples in a manner that defies explanation	Unconsciously does what normally works

Adapted from Mind Over Machine *by Dreyfus and Dreyfus.*

make them any more competent. They have begun to internalize the new skills and capabilities by developing the ability to go beyond simply applying rule-bound procedures in highly structured settings. Competent individuals apply tools and principles in a broad range of circumstances, adapting their practices to the specific situation through careful study of the context and selection among viable alternatives.

Proficient. Proficiency comes neither from more book learning nor from instructional sessions but from direct experience gained by continual practice in diverse settings. Proficient performers have internalized all the tools and concepts of the field and can reliably apply the tools and principles to any task or situation in a highly flexible and fluid manner. They intuitively grasp the whole of a situation without decomposing it into component features (through a process known as "holistic discrimination and association") and apply the appropriate set of skills. However, they still act based on a *conscious* decision-making process.

Expert. Experts generally know what to do based on mature and practiced understanding. They have fully internalized perception and action in their specific domain and do *both* intuitively, without conscious thought. An expert skier, for example, doesn't consciously study the terrain and strategize about the best path to follow or form to use—she just skis down the hill, making adjustments as needed. When things are proceeding normally, experts don't solve problems or make decisions; they just do what usually works. Experts often develop through mentoring relationships and apprenticeships, where they learn by absorbing new capabilities through continued exposure, observation, and interaction with an expert. Learning at this stage is often rooted in conversations and direct interaction with other experts. Doctoral programs for researchers and internships and residencies for medical doctors are examples of such institutionalized apprenticeships.

Five-Stage View of Systems Thinking

We can start to answer the questions we asked at the outset by walking through the five stages in the context of the core capabilities we saw in the three-legged stool diagram. In particular, we'll apply the model to the discipline of systems thinking to get a sense of the kinds of progressive steps an individual would need to take on the road to becoming an expert systems thinker.

Novice Systems Thinkers have a basic literacy in the tool of causal loop diagrams (CLDs). They know the rules for assigning either an "s" (causing a change in the **same** direction) or an "o" (causing a change in the **opposite** direction) to each link and can tell the difference between reinforcing and balancing loops. They can read simple diagrams created by others, but cannot yet construct a diagram on their own. Novice systems thinkers also know about systems archetypes and can describe what each archetype structure looks like as well as its corresponding pattern of behavior over time.

Advanced Beginner Systems Thinkers have mastered the basic mechanics of using links (s's and o's) and loops (reinforcing and balancing) and can map out simple loop structures. They use the systems archetypes as "templates" to recognize similar structures and dynamics playing out in their own settings. Advanced beginners also understand the basic lessons of systems principles (generalized observations about how complex systems behave, such as worse before better, unintended side-effects, and policy resistance). In addition, they can identify cases where systems principles prevail and anticipate when a systems principle applies to a specific situation. They are familiar with some basic stock and flow structures, such as the aging chain, co-flows, and anchoring-and-adjustment, and can identify similar structures in their own settings.

Competent Systems Thinkers have mastered the art of developing CLDs on topics they are familiar with and can map as many loops as necessary. They have fully internalized the systems archetypes and use them to understand complex dynamics in diverse settings. They also intuit when systems principles are relevant to a situation and think through the process of identifying the structures that are operating. Competent systems thinkers represent structures equally well in both CLDs and stocks and flows. They can convert those pen-and-paper conceptual models into computer simulation models and possess a solid working knowledge of basic computer modeling tools and skills. Because they themselves are so consciously aware of the tools and skills they are learning, individuals at the competent stage are also capable of teaching others how to draw CLDs, use systems archetypes, identify systems principles, and develop basic stock and flow structures to the level of an advanced beginner.

Being a highly seasoned and capable systems thinking consultant means one has reached at least the proficient stage.

Proficient Systems Thinkers view the world in terms of feedback loop structures and archetypal patterns. When they see profits falling, for example, they can't help but look at the situation in a larger context of other critical variables that affect profits. When they encounter a problem, they immediately sense the systemic implications and explore possible actions using mapping and computer tools to help sort through the multiple possibilities. In addition to mastering all the skills found at the competent level, proficient systems thinkers can consult to others and tackle issues in any setting. They intuitively grasp the important systemic structures in a situation and then select the appropriate actions to take. Being a highly seasoned and capable systems thinking consultant means one has reached at least the proficient stage.

Expert Systems Thinkers have elevated all the skills and knowledge from the previous stages to the intuitive level. They use systems thinking as a natural part of the creative process; the concepts and tools are inseparable parts of how they think and act. Experts do not consciously use a systems thinking tool or try to think in a particularly systemic way; they simply do what normally works, which happens to be systemic in its approach.

FIVE-STAGE VIEW OF BECOMING A SYSTEMS THINKER

	Domain of Event Training		Domain of Action Learning		
Skill Stage	**Novice**	**Advanced Beginner**	**Competent**	**Proficient**	**Expert**
Systems Thinking Skills and Tools	Causal loop diagrams (CLD), systems archetypes (SA)	CLD, SA, systems principles (SP), stocks and flows (S&F)	CLD, SA, SP, S&F, computer modeling (CM), teaching of basics	CLD, SA, SP, S&F, CM, teaching of basics, consulting skills	All known skills and tools
Internalization of Skills and Tools	Exposed and aware; able to apply in context-free settings	Recognizes and applies in structured settings	Internalizes and applies in more unstructured settings	Intuitive and applies consciously in all settings	Masters and applies unconsciously or tacitly in all settings
Formal Training Time†	2–5 days	5–10 days	20–30 days	As needed to address issues as they are encountered	All informal, mostly through conversations and interactions with other experts
Overall Time Frame w/ Active Practice†	1–2 months	3–6 months	12–18 months	1–3 years	5–10 years

†The times are specific to each stage and are in addition to the times indicated in the other stages. Also, the time frames shown are estimates that are meant to provide an order of magnitude reading rather than precise numbers for planning purposes. Many factors make the time frames longer or shorter for any specific individual.

The table called "Five-Stage View of Becoming a Systems Thinker" contains a summary of the stages for developing systems thinking skills and estimates of how much training and practice time are required to advance from stage to stage. The Novice and Advanced Beginner levels are based on the content delivered in most two- to five-day workshops currently offered by various organizations. The Proficient and Expert stages fall into the range of time required to earn a doctorate in the field of system dynamics. What is noteworthy about these time estimates is that *there are virtually no public programs yet available to systematically elevate a person to the Competent stage*. Hence there is no reliable way to build a level of competence within organizations, short of sending someone to a master's or PhD program.

The Case for Building Competence

The situation of developing organizational learning capabilities in most organizations is represented in "Outside Expertise vs. Internal Capability" on p. 38 by the two solid arrows at the top of the diagram. That is, companies invest in developing skills by using outside expertise to get people to a Novice or maybe an Advanced Beginner level. When those novices and advanced beginners fail to produce significant results through application of their new skills, many companies abandon the effort. But, if we hope to benefit from acquiring new organizational learning skills *as an organization,* we must be able to get a critical mass of people to at least the Competent level.

We are right back to the dilemma of learning calculus posed at the beginning of this article. Many organizations, for example, have dabbled in acquiring systems thinking skills and have sent people off to attend two- to five-day workshops. Most of these learners reach only a Novice level of capability, which does not produce many visible results. Sending them to additional workshops that are not coherently designed to build competence usually doesn't do much to develop their capabilities beyond an Advanced Beginner level. And, without a framework for assessing what level of skill a learner has reached, managers may think that they have invested more than enough resources in developing knowledge of the discipline and conclude that something is wrong with the discipline itself.

The challenge for many organizations is sustaining a level of commitment over time to developing a certain level of internal capability

OUTSIDE EXPERTISE VS. INTERNAL CAPABILITY

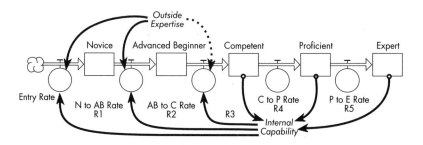

The solid arrows at the top show that companies invest in outside expertise to get people to a Novice or Advanced Beginner level. The challenge is using outside expertise to help people reach the Competent level (dotted arrow). They can then contribute toward developing others' capabilities (lower arrows).

and skill. One way of achieving this goal is to be more *strategic* in the use of outside expertise to help build internal competence in a systematic and measurable way (dotted arrow in "Outside Expertise vs. Internal Capability"). Once a core group of people has reached the Competent level, they can then apply what they know to produce better results for the organization and contribute toward developing others' capabilities. This way of internalizing and leveraging knowledge thereby creates an internally driven self-reinforcing engine of growth (the lower arrows in the diagram).

If an organization is serious about developing its ability to create its own future, it must find a way to help a critical mass of employees reach the Competent level in a skill or set of skills. Gaining awareness of the different levels of skill development, consciously formulating a plan to develop internal competence, and leveraging the talents of outside trainers are key ways for organizations to start developing the pillars of organizational learning capabilities on which they can create their futures. ⬿

Part Two

The Power
of Theory

*Although virtually every organization says that people are their most important assets, this proclamation is rarely supported by the infrastructures that exist. Instead of organizing in a way that taps into the **thinking** capacities of people, most organizations are designed around getting the most **doing** out of their people. In this section, we take a deeper look at what it means to commit to being an organization that is capable of continually generating new visions of its future and then creating the necessary knowledge to get there.*

If we want to create truly lasting changes, we must embed the changes in the deep infrastructures of our organization. For example, if we want everyone to be quality conscious, we need to embed that consciousness into the everyday systems and procedures people use. If we want an innovative culture, we need to create structures that make innovation a part of everyone's life, such as 3M's policy that everyone should devote a specific portion of their time to new product ideas. In other words, things should not be left to chance or cobbled together in an ad hoc way.

One of the critical requirements for any learning to occur is to have the space and the capacity to reflect on one's actions, decisions, and policies. Too often, however, we mistake creating temporary workarounds on the fly as real learning. The problem with even the best learnings is that without some kind of infrastructure for thinking things through and a way to codify the learning in a coherent

39

way, we often stay stuck in situational, fragmented, or opportunistic learning (as mentioned in the previous section). This is why we need to build learning infrastructures and to legitimize the role of theory building in our organizations.

"Building Learning Infrastructures" (p. 43) *is about approaching organizational learning (and knowledge creation) in the same way we would approach any serious initiative we want to embed in our organizations. We need time and space that will help us shift from working in the system to working on the system. It is only by stepping temporarily out of our day-to-day swirl of activities that we are able to see things from a broader and more detached perspective. What is needed is the manager's equivalent of a sports team's practice field in which to learn. Unfortunately, what we usually have are* performance fields*, where people are supposed to both perform and learn in real time. While one can argue that good teams can and do learn as they perform, most learning there is likely incremental rather than path-breaking. In other words, you won't see teams trying something they've never tried or practiced before in the middle of a real game. Yet, that is what we often expect our managers to do without the benefit of a practice field in which to think and test new learnings.*

In a way, organizational learning equals theory building. To paraphrase Dr. Deming's succinct observation of "No theory, no learning," I would say "No theory building, no organizational learning." What I mean by theory is exactly the dictionary definition of theory, namely, "systematically organized knowledge applicable in a relatively wide variety of circumstances, especially a system of assumptions, accepted principles, and rules of procedure devised to analyze, predict, or otherwise explain the nature or behavior of a specified set of phenomena."

Theory is the most practical thing we can focus on in our organizations, but unfortunately its vital link to everyday relevance has been lost, due to its association with "ivory towers" and isolated researchers asking esoteric questions.

But, if we recognize the importance of theory to virtually everything we do, we will see that the way we think and the way we see affect how we build theories of our world. Those theories, in turn, affect the way we see and think about the world. So, one of the first skills we will need to master is the ability to become aware of the way in which we create our worldviews. That is the focus of the article on **"Paradigm-Creating Loops: How Perceptions Shape Reality"** (p. 51).

The next article in this section, **"TQM and Systems Thinking as Theory-Building Tools"** (p. 59), *explores how these two powerful method-*

ologies offer concepts and tools that can help you strengthen your theory-building skills. For example, you can learn how to work with feedback loops, one tool of systems thinking, to articulate and refine your current operating theories. At the same time, while TQM and systems thinking draw on multiple theories, you can also see how all theories do have limitations that define the boundaries of their relevance.

*Finally, the last article of this section, **"What Is Your Organization's Core Theory of Success?"** (p. 69), takes a deeper look at how you can utilize systems thinking tools to build a better theory about how to take more effective actions. This article builds on the theme of this section by focusing on using theories in interventions, offering concrete examples that help you know when to step on the "accelerator" and when to slam on the "brakes." You also learn a comprehensive process for how to shift from a "parts" to a "loop" perspective through the detailed sidebar **"From Key Success Factors to Key Success Loops"** (p. 74).*

Chapter Four

Building Learning Infrastructures

"We have a lot of infrastructure in our organization for decision-making; we have very little infrastructure for learning."

—Bob Allen,
Chairman of AT&T

I n order to facilitate and accelerate learning, we need to design opportunities for making mistakes. While organizations have many fail-safe systems to ensure smooth operations, most companies have few "safe-failing" spaces to enhance learning.

Learning infrastructures create a process through which the assumptions of an organization are continually surfaced, challenged, and (if necessary) changed. Such structures are places in which corporate "sacred cows" are subject to scrutiny rather than accepted as truth, and where people develop and explore multiple future scenarios rather than focusing on a single plan.

For most organizations, such learning infrastructures do not exist. Yet they may be the single most important factor for creating sustained competitive advantage because they can provide an organization with the ability to continuously learn about itself. Learning infrastructures provide the means for an organization to develop its own theory (or set of principles) of how it works in a way that is comprehensible and actionable to all its members.

An Infrastructure for Working "on" the System
Building infrastructures for learning requires a parallel process that takes us out of day-to-day pressures into a different kind of space in which we

can practice and learn. With learning infrastructures, we are able to step out of the system so that we can work "on" it and not just "in" it.

There is an ongoing learning cycle that creates a bridge between the performance field (working in the system) and practice field (working *on* the system) (see "Parallel Learning Process" for an example of this learning cycle applied to the product-development process). The learning cycle of Observe-Assess-Design-Implement (O-A-D-I) links the two processes together: "Assess" and "Design" are emphasized in the practice field, and "Implement" and "Observe" are emphasized in the performance field.

Perhaps the most important link in the learning cycle lies in the "Observe-Assess" step, because our designs can be only as good as the assessments on which they are based. In turn, if our assessments are not grounded in actual observations, but in previously held assessments, then we are on shaky ground. The O-A-D-I learning cycle thus helps us to continually reflect on what we think we know and how we know it—in essence, to challenge our prevailing mental models.

This parallel process can be likened to a manager's equivalent of a practice field, which enhances his or her ability to perform "on-line" by creating an environment that is safe for experimentation and failures. As

PARALLEL LEARNING PROCESS

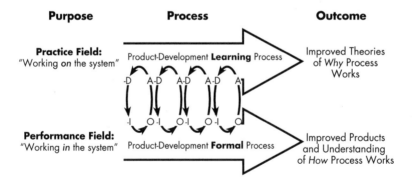

The O-A-D-I (Observe-Assess-Design-Implement) learning cycle links the practice and performance fields together in a continuous process of theory building and experimentation.

with a sports team, the practice field provides the tools and the appropriate arena for trying out new "plays" or strategies that may be radical departures from standard procedure.

A management flight simulator, for example, can be most useful for understanding situations in which causality is distant in time and space, or when the inherent time lag is particularly long (on the order of months or years) and organizational complexity is high. Management flight simulators are one of many tools that can be used in a practice field. Causal loop diagrams, systems archetypes, Action Maps, dialogue, and the Ladder of Inference are among the many other tools and frameworks that can also be utilized to enhance learning.

Creating learning infrastructures such as practice fields or learning laboratories is an important part of becoming a learning organization, but alone it is inadequate. It is too easy for such structures to become "training" infrastructures. There is nothing wrong with training per se. But training involves teaching a new twist on a well-established body of knowledge or disseminating that body of knowledge itself. Learning, on the other hand, requires a shift in the understanding of the base of knowledge itself. It is the difference between acquiring new information that fits into a current theory and developing a new theory. Learning infrastructures should help organizations build their own ongoing theories about how they work as a system.

Theory-Building Process

Because individuals are continually learning in organizations, one can argue that organizations are very supportive of learning. In most cases, however, the learning is done at an individual, not organizational, level. Oftentimes, there is no coherent process for integrating the learnings of many individuals into a form that can benefit the whole organization. In short, there is no theory-building process.

The word *theory* is too often viewed as an esoteric word that has no practical meaning. In fact, theory is of utmost practical importance because theories are distillations of our knowledge and understanding of the world. Theories represent the general principles drawn from a body of facts and observations. Without them, we could not learn because we would have no means to provide a coherent structure to our observations.

Given today's pace of change and organizational complexity, managers need to be competent in applying the research skills of a scientist to develop better theories about how their organizations work as a system. The old paradigm of feeding experiments from organizations into research institutions that then feed the results back is no longer adequate.

In *Beyond the Stable State*, Donald Schön pointed out that a major disruption in this paradigm occurred when the pace of change crossed into the intragenerational state—when lessons learned became obsolete within the same generation. Given this pace of change, the research cycle must be compressed, otherwise solutions (in the form of research results) will be stillborn—the problems that they addressed will no longer be relevant.

The Manager's New Roles: Researcher and Theory-Builder

In order to keep pace with intragenerational change, managers need to become *theory-builders* within their own organizations. It is no longer sufficient to apply generic theories and frameworks like bandages to one's own specific issues. As theory-builders, managers must have an intimate knowledge of how their organization works as a whole—but they also require some guiding theory and methodology to make sense of their experience and learning.

There is no "golden formula" that will hold for all time. Companies that lived by the learning-curve theory almost died by it (as in the case of Texas Instruments and the personal-computer debacle). Others who followed the Boston Consulting Group business-portfolio theory also had their share of problems. Theory building should therefore not be done as an academic exercise but as a process grounded in reality that continually helps provide a framework for interpreting one's competitive environment.

Theory-Building Loops

There were several projects being conducted at the MIT Organizational Learning Center (now the Society for Organizational Learning), which attempted to design and embed a theory-building process within an organization. By conducting parallel "experiments" at multiple company sites, researchers hoped to accumulate learnings across organizations that would allow each organization to accelerate its own learning. They thus were trying to integrate a variety of research methods that build theory at various levels (see "Organizational Theory-Building Cycle"). Although a lot of the Learning Center work lay in the (virtual) world of ideas, model formulation, and design of flight simulators and learning labs, an important aspect of the Learning Center's theory-building process was its close integration with active experimentation in several company sites.

The Learning Center research efforts can be viewed in terms of four interrelated learning loops which guide all projects—grounded theory building, dynamic theory building, behavioral decision theory building, and managerial practice-field theory building:

Grounded Theory Building (Loop L_1): This loop represents the field-research tradition of building theory based on observable data. It is

ORGANIZATIONAL THEORY-BUILDING CYCLE

The four theory-building loops integrate a variety of research methods to build theory at various levels.

rooted in direct observations, but instead of bringing preformulated frameworks that are then applied to the data, we try to hear what the facts themselves have to say.

Grounded theory building is an *inductive* process of suspending prior assumptions in order to view observable data through fresh eyes. Action science, clinical research, and ethnography are probably the most relevant research approaches. Mapping tools such as systems archetypes, causal loop diagrams, and Action Maps can play an important role in building grounded theory.

Dynamic Theory Building (Loop L_2): Static models can provide illuminating frameworks to help us understand our observations (e.g., supply and demand curves of economics), but they don't provide an opportunity to explore the rich set of dynamics that are possible over time. In dynamic theory building, we are interested in understanding how our grounded theories play out over time. This loop includes the traditional system dynamics model-building process of data collection, model formulation, testing, revising, and validation. It includes some of the work represented by loop L_1, but builds on it in a more rigorous fashion.

Behavioral Decision Theory Building (Loop L_3): People do not always behave rationally or in their own best interests, especially in complex dynamic environments where causality is separated in space and time. This theory loop attempts to understand why people make the decisions they do, in order to improve their decision-making in the future. MIT professor John Sterman's work on dynamic decision-making is a good representation of behavioral decision theory studies. Using interactive computer simulators to study how managers make decisions in a laboratory setting is one part of the work; linking the impact of those studies to actions in the workplace is another.

Managerial Practice-Field Theory Building (Loop L_4): Creating meaningful practice fields for managers requires an understanding of what makes a practice field "real" enough to be taken seriously and yet "playful" enough to provide a learning environment. Experiments can be conducted in the practice field that would not be possible in the actual work environment, and successive rounds of experiments can help an organization begin to develop its own organizational theory.

All four learning loops are important to organizational theory building. In the short term, no single project is likely to adequately address all four loops at once. But over time, the collection of various projects across many companies will help us build a rich set of theories about how organizations learn at multiple levels. The hope is that as more organizations engage in theory building, it will become such an embedded part of doing business that the alternation between practice and performance will be a seamless process of integrated learning. ⌒

———— ≈⟩ ————

Chapter Five

Paradigm-Creating Loops: How Perceptions Shape Reality

W

e are in the midst of an unprecedented upheaval—a fundamental shift in the structure and nature of business. According to *Fortune* magazine, "The greatest social convulsions of the years ahead may occur in the workplace, as companies struggling with fast-paced change and brutal competition reshape themselves—and redefine what it means to hold a job" ("A Brave New Darwinian Workplace," Jan. 25, 1993).

To respond to this changing paradigm, what is needed may not be a change of action, but a change in perception. How we think, act, and value are all associated with our particular view of reality. In order to create a new "reality," we must discover how our current worldview affects the way we perceive and respond to problems. The leverage lies in going to a more fundamental level—to look beyond the problems themselves and re-examine the paradigm that gave rise to them.

The Problem-Solving Model of Managing

The prevailing model of management can be described as a "problem-solution" model: We encounter problems, and as managers, we are expected to solve them as quickly as possible (see "Problem-Solution Model" on p. 53). In this model, we attack each problem individually, apply an appropriate solution, and then move on to the next one.

The problems rarely remain "solved," however. From a systems thinking perspective, we can see how solutions often feed back to create *other* problems, or even a repeat of the same problem. By the time this happens, it often appears to be a brand-new problem because we either have forgotten about the previous round of solutions, or the same person is no longer in that position (the average tenure in a position is 18 months or less in some companies). This creates a series of problem-solution cycles that can keep an organization continually busy fighting fires instead of taking more fundamental action.

How we think, act, and value are all associated with our particular view of reality. In order to adapt to and create a new "reality," we must discover how our current worldview affects the way we perceive and respond to problems.

At its worst, the problem-solution paradigm leads us to see problems in terms of predetermined solutions. Statements such as, "The problem is we need a better information system," or "The problem is we need the latest flexible manufacturing system," are examples of solution statements at work. The danger of this habit is that once we begin to frame problems in terms of solution statements, we exclude other possibilities—including the possibility that our original statement of the problem may be wrong.

Even when we don't resort to our favorite solution, we often don't challenge the problem statement itself. Problems are nothing more than a formal statement of a set of assumptions about the world. Those assumptions, however, are often not made explicit. By conversing and making decisions at the level of tacit assumptions, we can get very good at defending our point of view at the expense of learning. This can lead to what Chris Argyris of Harvard University calls "skilled incompetence." Rather than looking at the real data and real issues—which may prompt a re-articulation of the problem—we become very skilled at dancing around the issues.

Problem Articulation

To re-examine the way we think about problems and solutions, we need to understand more fundamentally what a problem is. In reality, there are no problems "out there" in the world—nature just *is*. Whether we see an event or situation as a problem depends on our view of the world. For example, if oil prices double, is that a problem? Americans' response would be a resounding "Yes!," since the U.S. economy is heavily dependent on petroleum products. Those living in an OPEC nation, however, would not see it as a problem at all. People living in an undeveloped country with no dependence on oil would probably not even be interested.

Problems do not exist independently of the person who sees them. Out of the pool of life we "construct" problems in our minds (or in our organizations) by the way we view reality (see "Problem Articulation"). Fred Kofman of Leading Learning Communities, Inc. suggests that deconstructing a problem and finding a way to re-articulate it can provide much more leverage than trying to just double our efforts to solve the

---

PROBLEM ARTICULATION

Problem-Solution Model

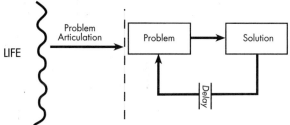

Balancing Problem Articulation and Problem Solving

Source: Fred Kofman

To an extent, we create the problems we see by the way we view reality, and how we articulate those problems can determine the future direction of our reality. To break out of the "problem-solution" model of reality, we need to go back one step further to re-examine the question, "How did we distill out of this vast pool of life a particular problem which led us to act a certain way?"

---

problem as it is currently stated. One of the clear challenges is to explore more explicitly how we articulate problems. *Why* do we consider something a problem? The "why" is what leads us to surface the deeper set of assumptions that may give insight into reformulating an entirely different problem.

Paradigm-Creating Loops

How can we break out of the problem-solving straitjacket and begin reframing issues in new ways? One tool that can help is the Ladder of Inference, developed by Chris Argyris. The Ladder of Inference provides a framework for exploring mental models. It graphically depicts the process we use to draw conclusive opinions and judgments from data, showing that individual evaluations are, in reality, highly abstract and inferential.

At the bottom of the Ladder of Inference is directly observable data: those things that can be objectively observed (see "The Reflexive Loop"). From that data, we add culturally shared meaning—that is, we

THE REFLEXIVE LOOP

The reflexive loop illustrates how our mental models can influence the way we view reality. We make leaps up the Ladder of Inference from data to values and assumptions, and then operate based on those assumptions as if they are reality. It can also be called the paradigm-creating loop, because it is the process through which, over time, we develop a shared set of cultural assumptions and values about how we view reality.

interpret and make sense of an event by the norms of our culture. For example, suppose Bob, a colleague, walked into a 9:00 meeting at 9:15. The directly observable data is that Bob physically entered the room 15 minutes after the scheduled start time. What do we say to ourselves when we notice this? When managers are asked this question, typical responses are:

>"He's late."
>
>"He doesn't care."
>
>"His previous meeting ran late."
>
>"He's not a team player."
>
>"He's disorganized."

If we locate the responses on the Ladder of Inference, we see that most of them are on the higher rungs of the ladder, reflecting judgments and values based on the observable data.

There is nothing inherently wrong about drawing inferences and conclusions from the events we observe. In fact, the ability to move quickly up the Ladder is what enables us to make sense of the incredibly complex, infinitely detailed world in which we live. It is impossible for us to see and absorb everything—we are constantly selecting out a narrow slice of life to focus on and understand. What we don't often realize, however, is that our beliefs and assumptions directly affect the selection process by which we receive new observable data. Argyris calls this process the reflexive loop because it happens subconsciously and involuntarily.

For example, if we have concluded that Bob doesn't really care about meetings and is not a team player, what do we begin to notice about Bob? We take note of all the times he shows up late and we ignore or aren't aware of all the times he is on time. We notice that Bob does not say much at meetings, but don't register the fact that a few people always dominate the conversation and that there are others who say even less than Bob. We continually filter out any information that doesn't fit in with the mental model we have created about Bob. In fact, *all* the data we see confirm our beliefs and assumptions about Bob. We have leapt from data up to beliefs and assumptions, and then operated as if the assumptions are the reality.

The reflexive loop can also be called the paradigm-creating loop, because it is the process through which, over time, we develop a shared set of corporate assumptions and beliefs about reality. In *The Machine That*

Changed the World (New York: Rawson Associates), there is a striking example of how this paradigm-creating process literally affects our ability to see. The book describes a new system of manufacturing invented by Toyota called "lean production" that uses less material, requires smaller inventories, has a shorter design time, and produces fewer defects than the traditional mass-production system. The authors tell the story of a General Motors plant manager's reaction after seeing a lean production plant in Japan: He "reported that secret repair areas and secret inventories had to exist behind the plant, because he hadn't seen enough of either for a 'real' plant." In actuality, there is no rework area in that plant—they drive the cars right off the assembly line and onto the ships. The GM manager's paradigm of a "real" plant kept him from seeing that there might be an alternative way to produce cars.

Mistaking the Map for the Territory

Comedian Steven Wright tells this joke: "Last summer my wife and I were planning our summer vacation. We bought a map of the United States. It was life-sized. One mile equals one mile. We never went on the vacation because it took the whole summer to fold the map."

Of course, buying a life-sized map is ridiculous—it would be no more useful than reality itself. A map is useful precisely because it is a simplification of reality. We would never mistake the map for the territory and plan a trip as if California is only three feet away from New York. And

---

VALUING DIVERSITY

Encouraging diversity has become a prime objective in many organizations. As a result, it is fast becoming an unquestionable belief—oftentimes without a real understanding of its importance. Why should we value diversity? The implications of the reflexive loop suggest that each person has a completely unique perspective on the world—not just in a philosophical sense, but grounded in the everyday experiences and worldview of the individual. In essence, the paradigm-creating loop is a world-creating loop. Each of us lives in an entirely unique world. We do have a great deal of overlap (i.e., culture), which allows us to interact and understand each other, but our uniqueness is a defining characteristic of who we are as an individual. Valuing diversity, then, allows us to access what each unique world has to offer. Having a diverse set of such worlds can create new possibilities and innovations that would otherwise not emerge.

---

yet we are prone to make such errors of perception whenever we mistake our mental models for the real world.

Marcel Proust once said, "The real voyage of discovery consists not in seeking new landscapes but in having new eyes." Becoming aware of how our view of the world is continually being constructed through the reflexive loop can prevent us from mistaking the map for the territory. Seeing problems as a product of our own thinking and not a product of nature can open our eyes to a whole new world of possibilities. ☞

Further reading: Chris Argyris, "Teaching Smart People How to Learn," *Harvard Business Review*, May/June 1991 (Reprint #91301).

Chapter Six

TQM and Systems Thinking as Theory-Building Tools

O ur brains are pattern-making systems—they organize our perceptions of the world into patterns that enable us to function effectively. For example, when we eat, our brain follows a particular set of patterns that guides the use of our fork and the amount of pressure we apply to our knife, without our having to think about and make decisions at each choice point. The simple fact that we can recognize the fork as a fork is a result of our pattern-making ability.

Edward de Bono, author of *Lateral Thinking* and *I Am Right, You Are Wrong,* likens the patterns in our brains to well-worn grooves. He explains that if we pour a teaspoon of hot ink over a plate of JELL-O™, the ink will dissolve parts of the gelatin as it flows over the surface and will form grooves. Any additional ink is likely to flow into the already-formed grooves and further deepen them. Our brain organizes and groups related pieces of information in the same fashion.

The grooves are not just passive receptacles of new information, however; they are active "channelers" of our perceptions into already-formed patterns. When customer orders fall, for example, that information gets channeled through the "beef up marketing" or "cut prices" groove in our brain. This process serves us well as long as those grooves are relevant for making sense of the situation. It is ineffective, however, in responding to new changes in the environment, since the new information is channeled into the same old pattern. Over time, it can actually lead to patterned blindness—the inability to see anything but the established pictures we already have in our brains.

TQM and the Learning Organization

If our current grooves affect both what we see and how we interpret what we see, how can we ever break out of this circular trap? How can we overcome our patterned blindness?

One way out of old patterns is through theory. Creating a new conceptualization of an issue can open our eyes to different possibilities by allowing us to let go of what we think we already know. Becoming a learning organization, for example, means being committed to continually asking the question, "How do we know what we know?"

This requires the ability to see old things in new ways and also to "see" things conceptually that we have not yet seen visually. That is the important role of theory—to see in the mind's eye what we have yet to experience or know. In that respect, theories are like windows into the unknown.

One way out of old patterns is through theory. Creating a new conceptualization of an issue can open our eyes to different possibilities by allowing us to let go of what we think we already know.

In the 1980s, TQM offered a new theory that helped cut fresh grooves into our thinking about people, systems, and management. But TQM was only one step in the journey toward improving organizational learning. Systems thinking is another important discipline that brings additional theories, tools, and methods for building learning capacity. Together, TQM and systems thinking can help organizations see beyond their patterned blindness and work toward building a better understanding of their own organizational capabilities and structures. By becoming theory-builders, managers can help their organizations become creators of their own future.

Patterned Blindness

At the turn of this century, craft producers of automobiles "knew" that costs were constant regardless of volume. Because of the meticulous, labor-intensive process used, the cost of producing the 100th car was more or less the same as for the first one. But mass production, with its economies of scale, dramatically altered the cost-volume relationship. By the 1920s, mass production had virtually wiped out the craft producers.

Likewise, in the early 1980s, the Japanese shattered the cost/quality trade-off myth with high-quality, low-cost products. In the process, they invented a new way of doing business—lean production—that was every bit as radical as the shift from craft to mass production. Those who could not adapt shared the fate of the craft producers: In the United States and elsewhere, whole industries were nearly decimated (steel, machine tools, motorcycles, video cameras, televisions, memory chips, etc.).

These are not examples of small, competitive ups and downs, in which poor decisions led to problems in one or two companies. In these cases, the fundamental basis of competition had shifted, requiring a radical change in perspective that some companies were unable to make. It is not that the new competitors kept the technology from the others; people simply could not recognize the implications of that shift because of the grooves in their brains—patterned blindness. (See the top of p. 56 for an example of this phenomenon in lean production.)

Problem Solving: Helping or Tampering?

Patterned blindness often operates in a disguised form—problem solving. How many times have we heard, "The problem is we need the latest flexible manufacturing system . . . The problem is we need more patient beds . . . The problem is we need more sales staff . . . The problem is . . . "? These are solution statements masquerading as problem statements, and they are products of our individual mental grooves.

When our thinking is entrenched in these types of solution responses, we do not bother looking for alternatives because the answer seems so clear. These grooves, in practice, embody our *theory* of the way the world works. We may think theory is an esoteric term that has no place in practical matters but, in fact, theory affects everything we see, think, and do. As Dr. Edwards Deming once said, "No theory, no learning."

Without theory, we cannot learn, because we cannot make sense out of the jumble of infinite stimuli that we are exposed to at every instant.

One of the ways Deming demonstrated his point about theory was by conducting illustrative experiments. Using a marble, a piece of paper, and a pen, for example, he showed how corrective actions intended to improve performance actually make things worse (see "The Marble Experiment: A Theory in Action"). Intuition says, "If there are deviations, take corrective actions." Statistical theory counters, "If a system is in control, do nothing." But in the absence of a clear theory, it is

---

THE MARBLE EXPERIMENT: A THEORY IN ACTION

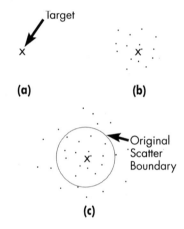

Deming used the following experiment to illustrate the usefulness of statistical theory: Place a target spot on a sheet of paper (a). Then take a marble, aim for the spot, drop the marble, and mark where it lands. After repeating the process several times, a cluster of marks will appear around the target spot (b).

Now make one change in the process. Instead of aiming for the target spot, try instead to compensate for the error of the previous drop. If, for example, your first marble drop was two millimeters to the north of the target, aim two millimeters south of the mark. It seems like a reasonable change in strategy. After all, if your gun sights were off, you could consistently compensate for it by adjusting your aim accordingly. Does this strategy actually help in the marble experiment? No. The pattern of dots gets bigger; the dispersion increases rather than decreases (c).

This result runs counter to our intuition that making adjustments should help us reach our goals, not make things worse. In fact, statistical theory suggests that if a system is within its limits, well-intentioned adjustments will actually take us further from our goal.

---

extremely difficult for most people to stand there and do nothing when it seems as if errors are being made.

Statistical Process Control

In the field of Total Quality, statistical theory was translated into a methodology called statistical process control (SPC). SPC provided a set of steps for distinguishing between special and common causes of variation. For example, control charts plotted with upper and lower limits around a target helped to identify the boundaries of a system's capability (see "Special vs. Common Causes"). Anything inside those boundaries was classified as "common" causes for which no corrective action was necessary. Points outside those limits were identified as "special" causes, meaning something had happened that was uncharacteristic of that system and needed to be investigated further. Special causes could be addressed by working within the existing system, but the common causes could be addressed only by changing the system itself.

Prior to the arrival of SPC, helpful "adjustments" like those in the marble experiment were actively being carried out in most manufacturing

---

SPECIAL VS. COMMON CAUSES

Upper Control Limit

Common Cause

Lower Control Limit

Special Cause

Special causes lie outside both the upper and lower control limits and are dealt with by working within the current system. But because common causes lie within the control limits, addressing them requires a change in the system itself.

---

operations. If, for example, you wanted a rod whose length was 30mm ± .1mm, and it came out larger or smaller, you naturally adjusted the calibration on the machine. In the absence of statistical theory with which to interpret the data, people would implement solutions (make adjustments) that actually increased the problem (greater deviations) and justified further corrective actions (more adjustments). That is, the solutions themselves guaranteed the need for more of the same solutions in the future.

Working with Multiple Theories

The application of SPC to manufacturing operations resulted in great success because the theory was well suited for controlling processes that are governed by physical laws and relationships. But statistics become less useful when we venture into the domain of social systems because many of the assumptions about predictability, repeatability, and linearity are not as appropriate. Therefore, as the use of TQM methods became more widespread, they were applied to a wider range of settings with decreasing levels of success.

Because social systems do not behave like mechanical and electrical systems, applying theories and tools better suited for the latter is not likely to enhance our understanding of the former. This does not mean that the theory behind TQM methods was wrong; it simply means that we reached the limits of their usefulness.

All theories have limits that define the boundaries of their relevance. Newtonian physics, for example, was not proven "wrong" when Einstein developed his relativistic view of the world. Einstein's theory of relativity simply defined the boundaries in which Newtonian physics worked and where it broke down. When you begin to approach the speed of light, Newtonian concepts of time and distance can no longer be treated as constants, but as relative concepts that are very much dependent on the reference frame from which you are making the measurements. For our day-to-day needs, however, Newton's laws adequately approximate reality.

In some of his later writings, Deming acknowledged the limited role of statistics in the larger arena of organizational transformation. He identified three other theories that were important: systems theory, psychology, and theory of knowing. He believed that the set of four were essential for developing what he called "profound knowledge." In his book *The

Fifth Discipline, Peter Senge presented five disciplines—shared vision, personal mastery, team learning, mental models, and systems thinking—that embody a range of theories about how to develop the capabilities of a learning organization.

Both Deming's and Senge's approaches draw on multiple theories, and both highlight the importance of understanding systems. In fact, systems thinking plays a particularly important role in organizational learning because the tools and methods of system dynamics enable you to not only be a user and interpreter of theory, but also an active theory-builder. And theory building is essential to building organizational learning.

Feedback Loops as Theory-Building Tools

System dynamics, the theoretical underpinning of systems thinking, allows us to articulate causal interconnections so that we can take high-leverage action instead of being paralyzed by complexity. System dynamics, which is grounded in feedback systems and control theory, provides a set of tools and methods for making sense of complex interconnections—similar to how TQM helped us understand variation through statistical theory. With respect to learning, TQM proved particularly strong in operational learning—building greater understanding of *how* to do things—while systems thinking is relatively strong in conceptual learning—developing richer theories about *why* things work the way they do.

In the systems thinking toolkit, there are two types of feedback loops we can use to build our own causal theories of organizational behavior—reinforcing and balancing. A reinforcing loop represents a process where a change in one direction is continually amplified in the same direction. In a balancing loop, a change in one direction produces a response that will try to take the system in the opposite direction. It is basically a control loop.

Causal Loop Theory Building

With these two basic types of loops, we can construct rich theories about the causal interrelationships that drive our organizational behavior. Causal loop diagrams not only provide a language for representing dynamic structures, but they also provide a way for us to make explicit and share the individual views of the world that govern our actions. By surfacing our individual assumptions about our organizations, we can work toward building a coherent and consistent working theory about our organization and our environment.

For example, one theory you may have is that increasing levels of feedback to employees will lead to increased performance over time, which leads to even more feedback (R1 in "Performance-Feedback Theory"). The pattern of behavior suggested by this loop is one of exponential growth. This is a testable theory. Data collection may reveal that

PERFORMANCE-FEEDBACK THEORY

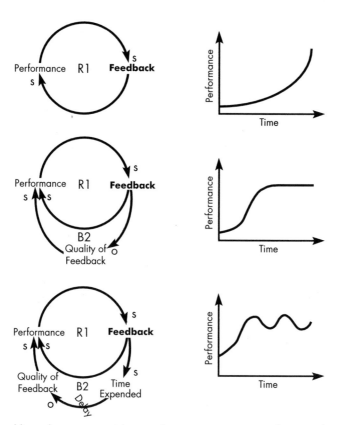

Causal loop diagrams provide us with a means to construct theories about dynamic relationships. For example, we may theorize that increasing feedback will improve performance over time (R1), or that an increase in feedback may actually decrease performance, depending on the quality of feedback (B2). Statistical tools can then help us test the validity of these theories.

performance rises initially, but after a while it plateaus. Someone else may suggest that performance can actually decrease if the quality of feedback is low, and that increasing feedback may actually lead to a decrease in the *quality* of the feedback (B2). A third person may add that it is not the increasing feedback that leads to lower quality of feedback, but the amount of time expended in giving feedback. As the time expended increases beyond a certain point (indicated by a delay), the quality of feedback suffers.

This example describes the beginnings of a theory about how feedback and performance are linked. Working through this as a team can reveal our collective understanding of what we think is going on in our organization. Causal loop diagrams and systems archetypes therefore provide us with a way to *construct* our theories; statistical tools can help us test the validity of the causal connections we have identified. In this way, both systems thinking and TQM are essential to the theory-building process.

Cutting New Grooves with Theory

Buckminster Fuller used to say that we start with the universe, and then recognize that any distinctions from then on are entirely arbitrary. In other words, the boundaries that we draw are not a product of nature but of our thoughts. Thus, theory plays a critical role in how we create the conceptual patterns through which we see our world and how susceptible we are to patterned blindness.

If we view the world through our theories (or patterns in our brains) then by becoming active theory-builders we can greatly enhance the learning capacity of our organizations. Systems thinking and TQM provide a complementary set of theories and tools for developing an organization's theory-building capabilities. Our ability to develop new theories will allow us to get out of existing grooves in thinking, to envision a whole different future, and then to take the necessary steps toward creating that future. That is the exciting promise and potential of organizational learning.

≈

What Is Your Organization's Core Theory of Success?

Managers in today's organizations are continually confronted with new challenges and increased performance expectations. At the same time, they are bombarded by a bewildering array of management ideas, tools, and methods that promise to help them solve their organizational problems and improve overall performance. Desperate to find solutions to intractable problems, beleaguered managers may succumb to the lure of new techniques and approaches that promise easy answers to tough issues. When they try the latest management fad, however, they find that the relief is only temporary; the same issues resurface later, perhaps in another part of the organization.

Managers often don't have the time, perspective, or framework to learn from the successes and failures of their problem-solving efforts. As a result, organizations fall into a recurring pattern of temporary relief followed by a return of the same problems. If people do attempt to learn from the past, they frequently find themselves ill prepared to make sense of their own experience. Even in cases where the solutions produce lasting results, managers often lack an understanding of why these approaches succeeded.

Limitations of Traditional Approaches

When attempting to determine why an initiative succeeded, most managers talk in terms of the individual factors they believe were critical to the success. This propensity to focus on factors in isolation rather than seeing them as interrelated sets is part of what Barry Richmond of High

Performance Systems refers to as "traditional business thinking." Indeed, many companies formulate their thinking about success as lists of important attributes or competencies, without identifying the key ways in which the items are connected.

For example, companies often begin their efforts to improve their organizations by listing critical success factors. They identify a goal (for example, industry leadership) and then list the factors that management agrees are essential to achieving this goal (such as desirable products and services, or ability to deliver). They then prioritize the items on the list and assign the top priorities to special teams.

This list-based approach poses several problems. First, people frequently treat the factors separately, in a "divide and conquer" strategy. The danger here is that they may not properly consider important *interactions* among the different factors. Hence, a marketing department may not warn manufacturing and customer service about the potential impact of a major marketing campaign.

Responsible leaders should ask themselves, "What good theories do we have that provide practical guidance for ensuring our organization's future success?"

Another problem is that if management reduces the initial investments after a key success factor (KSF) has reached a certain desired level, the success may prove temporary. Often, when we have achieved a certain desired level with KSF1, we declare victory and shift resources over to KSF2. As we build up KSF2 and then KSF3, KSF1 starts to deteriorate because of lack of continued investments. So, we shift some resources back to KSF1 as we declare victory on KSF2 and KSF3.

Unless managers develop a theory of how these factors are interrelated in creating ongoing success (or failure), they cannot put the data from their experiences together in a way that serves as a guide for future actions. Unfortunately, most approaches to helping organizations solve persistent problems focus on applying other people's theories and methods to the organization and not on developing a specific theory about the organization's own operations. Systems thinking and organizational learning can offer tools and methods for companies to begin developing such theories and for putting them into action.

The Importance of Theory

Regrettably, the corporate world has little appreciation for the importance and power of theory. Many managers associate theory with universities and research institutions, which they view as too insulated from the real world. Hence, managers often dismiss theory as too academic and irrelevant to the pragmatic conduct of business. But the *American Heritage Dictionary*, Standard Edition, defines theory as *"systematically organized knowledge applicable in a relatively wide variety of circumstances, especially a system of assumptions, accepted principles, and rules of procedure devised to analyze, predict, or otherwise explain the nature or behavior of a specified set of phenomena."* This definition clearly shows that there is nothing strictly academic about the concept of theory at all.

Using this definition of theory, we can say that creating a long-lived, successful organization means managers must develop systematically organized knowledge that represents the system of assumptions, accepted principles, and procedural rules they use to make sense of their past experience and to predict the future. In this sense, theory building is about developing a better understanding of our organizations and improving our capacity to predict the future. In other words, theory building has *everything* to do with running a successful business.

We have to be cautious when we use the word "prediction," because it tends to be used synonymously with the word "forecast." Forecasting attempts to provide a specific kind of prediction; however, it usually focuses on calculating specific numerical data that we expect to occur at some point in the future. The main criterion of success for forecasts is the accuracy of the forecasted result, not the accuracy of the assumptions or the methods used to produce it.

When we talk about predictions based on theory, however, we are more interested in the accuracy of the underlying assumptions and less in the numerical accuracy of the predicted result. Why? Because, in a complex world that is inherently unforecastable (a basic tenet in the emerging science of chaos), only understanding interrelationships can guide us in making the course corrections inevitably required in an environment of rapid and continual change. All good theories therefore help provide guidance by increasing our predictive power about the future.

Theory Building: Shifting from Factors to Loops

So, responsible leaders should ask themselves, "What good theories do we have that provide practical guidance for ensuring our organization's future success?" The more clearly you can articulate your organization's theories about what leads to success, the more deliberate you can be about investing in the elements that are critical to that success. From a systems thinking perspective, having a core theory of success means moving beyond identifying individual success factors to seeing the linkages that create the reinforcing engines of success within the organization.

For example, once we have a list of key success factors, we can take the next step of identifying how each KSF is connected to a reinforcing loop (see "Shifting to a Loop Perspective"). The key success loop (KSL) identified in our example shows that by increasing desirable products and services, we increase sales revenues and boost the amount of money available for investment. With more money to invest, we can draw more technical talent and produce even more desirable products and services (R loop).

Shifting our formulation of theories from factors to loops is important for several reasons. First, it forces us to think through the logical chain of causal forces that ensure that the KSF becomes self-sustaining. Second, it shifts our emphasis away from the factor itself to the broader set of interrelationships in which it is embedded. Third, by mapping each of our KSFs into key success loops, we are more likely to see the interconnections among all the KSFs. This approach requires shifting our worldview from one that sees *factors* as the lowest unit of analysis to one that recognizes *loops* as the basic building blocks of organizational systems. (For a step-by-step process you can work with, see sidebar "From Key Success Factors to Key Success Loops" on p. 74.)

Theory as an Intervention Guide

Having an explicit theory of success allows an organization to continually test the impact of planned actions and assess whether these actions are having a net positive or negative effect on the company's overall success. So, what might a theory of success look like in a learning organization?

SHIFTING TO A LOOP PERSPECTIVE

From Key Success Factor . . .

. . . To Key Success Loop

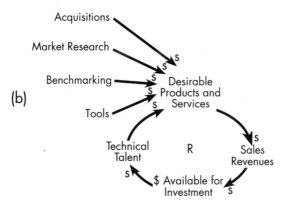

A key success factor is connected to a reinforcing loop. Here, as the number of desirable products and services increases, sales revenues and money for investment rise. As investments are made to increase technical talent, the ability to produce even more desirable products and services increases.

One such core theory of success would be based on the premise that as the quality of the relationships among people who work together increases (high team spirit, mutual respect, and trust), the quality of thinking improves (people consider more facets of an issue and share a greater number of different perspectives) (see "A Core Theory of Success" on p. 78). When the level of thinking is heightened, the quality of actions is also likely to improve (better planning, greater coordination, and higher commitment). In turn, the

FROM KEY SUCCESS FACTORS TO KEY SUCCESS LOOPS

Many of us are familiar with the following drill: Corporate pushes a new program, and each department must come up with its own plans for making the initiative a success. We start by brainstorming a list of Key Success Factors (KSFs) that are critical to implementing the new program (see "Traditional Key Success Factor Approach"). We then prioritize the KSFs and assign each to a team charged with bringing that KSF to a target level. Each team identifies a set of investments needed to reach the desired goal and then works toward meeting the objective. When the KSF hits the goal, the team declares victory and moves on to the next KSF on the list. Yet the larger program fails to achieve its overall goals.

TRADITIONAL KEY SUCCESS FACTOR APPROACH

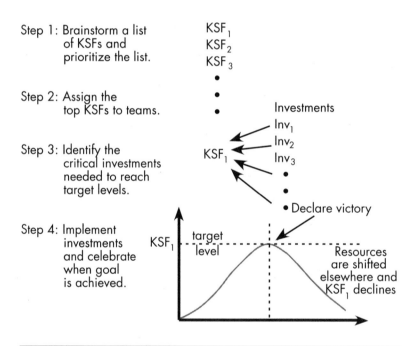

Step 1: Brainstorm a list of KSFs and prioritize the list.

Step 2: Assign the top KSFs to teams.

Step 3: Identify the critical investments needed to reach target levels.

Step 4: Implement investments and celebrate when goal is achieved.

KSF_1
KSF_2
KSF_3

Investments
Inv_1
Inv_2
Inv_3

KSF_1

Declare victory

KSF_1 target level

Resources are shifted elsewhere and KSF_1 declines

The Paradox of KSFs

Most of us approach a large, complex issue by breaking it down into manageable parts. By focusing on a few aspects at a time, we sometimes succeed in improving the parts, but we often fail to address the problem as a whole. In the long run, this approach robs us of resources that we could have used to look at an issue from a systemic perspective.

We can find ample evidence of the limits to a factors approach in medical literature. In Sweden, for example, researchers tried to reduce cardiovascular risk factors in 3,490 business executives. After five years of intervention and 11 years of follow-up, the executives had reduced their risk factors by an average of 46 percent, yet they had a higher death rate than members of a control group. A similar study in the United States produced comparable results.

We might dismiss these studies as statistical flukes if the consequences weren't so serious. The sad reality is that these results probably reflect many of our efforts, not just in healthcare but in virtually every facet of our organizations. Although we focus time and again on improving single factors, we fail to acknowledge that the health of most individuals—and most systems—is greatly determined by the relationships among critical loops. The line "the operation was successful, but the patient died" sums up the pitfalls of the factors approach to complex systems.

Beyond Factors to Loops
To create long-lasting success, we need to extend our factors approach and identify the interrelationships among the factors that drive the dynamics of the system—in short, to identify the Key Success Loops (KSLs). When we take a systemic approach, we realize that the lowest meaningful units of analysis are loops, not individual factors—and we no longer initiate actions on any factors until we distinguish the critical loop or loops involved.

Now, imagine being given the same charge as before from corporate (see "Key Success Loop Approach" on p. 76). We begin in the same way, by brainstorming and then prioritizing KSFs (Step 1). But instead of leaping into action by assigning the factors to teams, we take each of the high priority factors and identify at least one reinforcing loop that will make the factor self-sustaining without continued external investments (Steps 2 and 3). We integrate all of the loops into a single diagram, in which the individual loops are connected by the factors they have in common (for example, B and D in Step 4). We then look at the diagram as a whole and decide where to make the investments that would help support the success of the entire system (Step 5). Only after we have developed a sufficient understanding of the system will we assign teams to implement specific success loops. Each team then collaborates closely with those teams whose loops are directly connected to theirs (Step 6).

Launching a New Venture
Let's walk through a simplified example of a Key Success Loop approach. Suppose we want to launch a new business venture in our organization (see "New Business Venture Success Loops" on p. 77). We begin by brainstorming a list of KSFs that we believe are important to our success, such as number of new products, skilled people, profits, and ability to meet customer needs (Step 1).

We then focus on the first factor and try to identify a key loop that would make it self-reinforcing. We can ask either "What would an increase

continued on next page

continued from previous page

in the number of new products cause?" or "What would be an important driver of growth in the number of new products?" The first question leads us downstream in the arrow flow to "Revenues," while the second takes us in the upstream direction to "Acquisitions." Either way, we try to create a reinforcing loop around the original factor (Step 2). We then repeat the process with the remaining factors (Step 3).

After we have created a loop for each KSF, we look for common variables in the individual loops. In this example, loops R1 and R2 can be linked through "Revenues" and "# of New Products" (Step 4). Once we have a diagram that maps the key linkages, we can begin to identify the best places to make high-leverage investments (Step 5). Now we are

---

KEY SUCCESS LOOP APPROACH

Step 1: Brainstorm a list of KSFs and prioritize the list.

Step 2: Start with the top-priority KSF and identify a reinforcing loop that will be self-sustaining.

Step 3: Repeat Step 2 with all the high-priority KSFs.

Step 4: Try to integrate all the loops into a single diagram.

Step 5: Identify where to make investments in the context of the whole diagram.

Step 6: Assign teams to implement specific loops and collaborate with other teams.

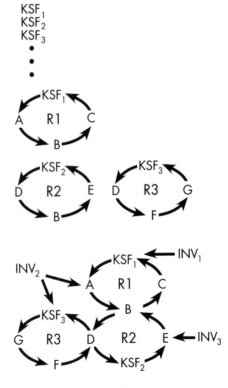

---

ready to assign teams to focus on each of the loops through a collaborative effort in which each team understands its loop in the context of the larger system (Step 6).

Benefits of KSLs

Moving beyond Key Success Factors to Key Success Loops offers a number of advantages. First, because the loop approach links you to a broader set of variables, you reduce the risk of focusing on the wrong factors. Even if you initially pick the wrong factors, the process of mapping the loops increases the likelihood that you will include the most important ones. Also, identifying the loops decreases competition for limited resources. When everyone can see the interconnections, teams are less likely to "pump up" their own factors without regard for the effect on others. Loops can also provide a clearer picture of where investing in one point could positively affect multiple factors. Finally, rather than being stuck in the "Ready, Fire, Aim" syndrome that many organizations experience, emphasizing KSLs can actually give you a viable "Ready, Aim, Fire" approach.

NEW BUSINESS VENTURE SUCCESS LOOPS

Step 1: Key Success Factors
    1) # of New Products
    2) Skilled People
    3) Profits
    4) Ability to Meet Customer Needs

Step 6: Assign each loop to a team, making sure that team members understand the loop in the context of the larger system and that they coordinate with other teams.

---

quality of results increases as well. Achieving high-quality results as a team generally has a positive effect on the quality of relationships, thus creating a virtuous cycle of better and better results.

The most important point about this kind of systemic theory is that success is not derived from any one of the individual variables that make up the loop, but rather *from the loop itself*. All of the variables are important for the theory to work properly, because if one of them isn't functioning, the reinforcing process doesn't exist. If we believe that this loop describes a relevant theory of success for our organization, it forces us to pay attention to how *all* the variables are doing and how each is affecting the others in the loop.

As an example, we can use this core theory of success to trace the implications of a common occurrence in corporations—top-down organizational efforts to get quick, short-term results. When results fall short of expectations, management often "helps" the people below by undertaking efforts intended to improve the bottom line immediately (see "Applying the Accelerator and the Brakes"). The "accelerator" (say, downsizing) works and improves the quality of results we are looking for (better profit picture). But those same actions can also serve as "brakes," or unintended consequences that counteract any beneficial actions. These actions can destroy the quality of relationships by creating mistrust

---

A CORE THEORY OF SUCCESS

As the quality of relationships rises, the quality of thinking improves, leading to an increase in the quality of actions and results. Achieving high-quality results has a positive effect on the quality of relationships, creating a reinforcing engine of success.

APPLYING THE ACCELERATOR AND THE BRAKES

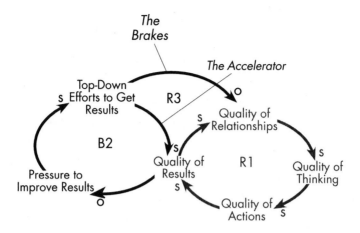

Management often undertakes efforts to get quick results. This "accelerator" improves the quality of results over the short term. But those same actions can also serve as "brakes" by destroying the quality of relationships and ultimately decreasing the quality of results.

and low morale, and thus ultimately decrease the quality of results. The end result may be a lot of wasted energy with no real improvement in overall results.

Without having a core theory, we might simply focus on the "accelerator" aspect of the intervention and declare victory when the results improve in the short term. We wouldn't necessarily connect the long-term negative consequences of the "braking" action to the original intervention. When the results deteriorate again, the pressure to improve results increases. We might respond by repeating the same efforts that we believe worked so well the last time. By having the theory and the accompanying loop, on the other hand, we can see how the top-down efforts may have a negative impact and implement additional measures to counterbalance that effect.

To illustrate how this generalized accelerator-and-brakes dynamic might play out in a specific situation, let's look at an example. Curtis Nelson, president and CEO of Carlson Hospitality Worldwide (the parent company of Radisson Hotels), wrote in their company magazine: "Take care of your people, inspire them, allow them to grow to their full potential and evoke their personality, and they will reach a higher level of job satisfaction. That in turn inspires greater commitment, which leads to greater guest satisfaction."

Although Nelson did not draw a loop in his article, he articulated in words his core theory of success for this hotel and cruise business (see "Hotel Core Success Loop"). The diagram shows that investments in people's potential enhances job satisfaction, which builds commitment and translates into higher guest satisfaction and higher revenues. An increase in revenues means a rise in profits, which leads to more investments in people.

Now, suppose something unexpected happens to decrease profits, such as a rise in airfares that reduces business travel. Top management might respond by calling for cost-cutting measures to improve the profit picture. In the short term, profits are likely to rise—the intended result. However, an unintended consequence of enacting such measures may be substantial decreases in the company's investment in its people, leading to a decrease in job satisfaction. This decrease in job satisfaction will reduce profits in the longer term, because employees will be less committed, causing a decline in customer satisfaction. Lower profits would

HOTEL CORE SUCCESS LOOP

Investment in people enhances job satisfaction and commitment, leading to higher guest satisfaction, revenues, and profits. Cost-cutting measures may cause profits to rise in the short term but fall over the long term, as employee commitment, customer satisfaction, and revenues decline.

then provoke another wave of cost cutting, repeating the accelerator-and-brakes dynamic. In this way, a one-time disturbance from the outside can trigger an internal response that keeps cycling for a long time.

Again, by articulating our core theory of success, we will be more likely to pay attention to both the short-term and the long-term consequences of our actions. In particular, our theory can prevent us from inadvertently undermining the very loop we depend on for our success.

Of course, in a real company setting, a core theory of success is likely to involve many loops, not just one. The various loops will be interconnected in many ways, and their dynamic behavior will not always be intuitively obvious. Building and understanding such theories requires more than a one-time investment in creating a quick overview map (like the ones in this article); it requires a shift in mindset that values theory building as a vital ongoing activity of the organization.

Managers as Researchers and Theory-Builders

But in order to survive and thrive in the emerging economic order, organizations must focus on producing long-term, sustainable results. Managers at every level need a broader perspective—a theory—of how their organization can create and maintain success. Theory building can no longer be seen as a separate activity from the practice of management—it must become an integral part of a manager's job. Managers must take on new roles as researchers and theory-builders, which will require investment in the development of new skills and capabilities. Just as we currently depend on accountants and financial statements to help us manage our complex enterprises, there may come a time when we will depend on our theory-builders and organizational maps and models to navigate the turbulent waters of tomorrow's business environment. ⌐

Part Three

A Systemic
Approach to
Creating Enduring Change

Most organizations seem to have gotten the message that building a shared vision is a desirable thing—or at the very least, a "fashionable" thing—to do. Unfortunately, many approach the visioning process much in the same reductionistic way they do everything else. Rather than see the shared vision work in the larger context of the organization's many interdependencies, organizations often treat it as another separate task to complete as quickly and efficiently as possible. So, many an organization goes through their traditional "roll-out" process, and everyone goes through the motions of participating in the latest management-fad activity—producing a lot of "sound and fury, signifying nothing."

If we are interested in creating enduring change, what we need is a very different theory about building shared commitment and vision to produce lasting results. We need to take a systemic view of the larger change process and cultivate both a wide and deep understanding of where we want to go (desired future reality) and be able to talk honestly about where we are (current reality). We also need to shift from the cascading top-to-bottom approach to one of multidirectional engagement at all levels. Building true shared vision operates on a theory of maximum engagement through a process of sharing one's own passionate vision, inviting others to articulate their own, and trusting the process to work without the need to overcontrol.

As important as theory is, however, we also need to support it with good methods and tools to operationalize and test the theory. To this end, **"Vision Deployment Matrix: A Framework for Large-Scale Change"** (p. 85) offers a guiding framework and method for creating an organizationwide shared vision. The matrix offers a more comprehensive roadmap for traversing the "chasm" that lies between the current reality of today's crises and the desired future's vision captured in ambitious corporate vision statements. By developing a collective understanding of the territory, we put ourselves in a much better position to reach our desired future.

One of the advantages of using this tool in a visioning process is that it provides a place to which virtually everyone can connect—because people have a natural tendency to think at different levels of perspective. Rather than arguing for one level to be the "right" one, many teams have discovered how their individual perspectives all contribute toward painting a fuller picture of their desired or current reality. It also provides a way to differentiate between different types of actions and why they might be more effective in one instance and less effective in another instance. This has to do with the concept of action modes, and how actions are most effective when their modality is matched to their appropriate level.

A central part of the VDM framework is the concept of seeing both our desired future and our current reality at multiple levels of perspective— Vision, Mental Models, Systemic Structures, Patterns, and Events. The two articles that follow, **"From Event Thinking to Systems Thinking"** (p. 93) and **"Levels of Perspective: 'Firefighting' at Multiple Levels"** (p. 99), provide additional insights into the specific uses of the Levels of Perspective as a tool for both more effective reflection and action. The framework itself serves as a balancing force against the dangers of getting stuck in just telling war stories at the event level—without ever rising to a higher level and higher leverage actions.

~

Vision Deployment Matrix™: A Framework for Large-Scale Change

"Many 'motivational experts' point to the Apollo space programme as a prime example of a mission motivated by an important vision. From this example they claim that all we need is a vision, and we, like those who created the Apollo programme, would be driven to higher and higher levels of performance. What they miss is that it mattered to the men and women who were in the programme that we reach the moon. Material or emotional return on investment did not motivate them. Because they authentically cared about the goals of the Apollo programme they were able to learn what they needed to learn, even when it was inconvenient, disappointing, frustrating, and sometimes heartbreaking."

—Robert Fritz,

Corporate Tides

Vision can be a powerful force for action when it is clearly artic-ulated and there is a genuine desire to bring it into reality. Yet many visioning efforts fail to bring about the desired results. Many organizations that catch the vision "fever" believe the job is fin-ished once a small group of top managers produce a vision statement and announce it to the rest of the organization. Expecting that the vision statement in and of itself will produce transformation, the initial group often disregards the importance of the process that brought about the commitment. When misinterpreted in this way, vision becomes a thing that people are expected to buy into, rather than a lively process of sharing what we most care about in a way that creates enthusiasm and shared commitment.

"People Resist Change"

When efforts to roll out a vision statement are met with resistance or produce no tangible results, we often conclude that "people resist change." In many organizations, this has become a corporate maxim that is often accepted without challenge. As organizations undertake change efforts—whether visioning, TQM, re-engineering, or something else—much discussion and effort is usually devoted to dealing with people who are resistant to change. How do we persuade them to go along with the plan? What incentives can we use to entice them to buy in?

Rather than spending time formulating strategies to deal with these "unchangeable" people, we should step back and ask ourselves, "Do they really exist?" When invited to participate in creating something they *truly care about*, people are usually more than willing to change—and sometimes they are even impatient with the larger organization's inability to move fast enough toward the goal. Most people do not resist change; they resist *being changed* when it is imposed from the outside.

The Chasm

Designing a process for involving people in sharing a vision is only one part of the formula for success. Visioning also requires a commitment to articulating current reality with clarity and honesty—talking about daily events as they really are, not as we wish them to be. In between vision and current reality lies an enormous "chasm" that we must cross in order to realize the desired future.

Many change efforts fail to achieve expected results because they do not strategically address ways to bridge the "chasm." Successfully managing large-scale organizational change requires a comprehensive, broad-based approach. To bridge the gap between future and current reality, we need to be explicit about the multiple levels on which we must think and act: events, patterns of behavior, systemic structure, mental models, and vision.

Vision Deployment Matrix

The Vision Deployment Matrix offers a schema for strategically planning how to cross the "chasm" between current reality and vision by painting a comprehensive picture of the desired future reality and current reality at five levels of perspective (see "Vision Deployment Matrix"). The Vision Deployment Matrix is meant to help everyone in the organization understand the current reality, the desired future reality, the gaps between the two, and the actions that should be taken to close the gap. This includes translating the ideals of a vision into a practical reality that guides and affects not only the strategic thinking in the organization, but the day-to-day operations as well.

To see how the Vision Deployment Matrix can be used to plan a large-scale change process, let's look at the healthcare industry, and "fill in" the matrix as we create a possible action plan for achieving a new vision of healthcare.

Start at the Vision level of Desired Future Reality. Beginning with the desired future reality is desirable because it allows us to be expansive

---

VISION DEPLOYMENT MATRIX

Level of Perspective (Action Mode)	Desired Future Reality	Current Reality	Gaps, Open Issues, and Questions	Action Steps	Indicators of Progress	Timeline
Vision (Generative)	Corporate Vision Statements					
Mental Models (Reflective)						
Systemic Structures (Creative)	THE CHASM					
Patterns (Adaptive)						
Events (Reactive)		Daily Crises				

(Increasing Leverage — shown along the left vertical axis)

The Vision Deployment Matrix offers a schema for strategically planning how to cross the "chasm" between current reality and vision by painting a comprehensive picture of the desired future reality and current reality at each level of perspective.

in our thinking and not get bogged down by current reality. It also frames the effort in terms of creating "what we want" rather than eliminating "what we don't want."

In the healthcare industry, for example, one vision of the future that has been articulated is "the creation of healthier communities."

Move down the multiple levels of Desired Future Reality. Staying with our focus on the desired future reality, we can flesh out what the vision means at each level by asking the following questions:

Mental Models: "What are the beliefs and assumptions that will be congruent with the vision?"

Systemic Structures: "How can we create structures that will be consistent with those beliefs?"

Patterns of Behavior: "What patterns of behavior do we want the structures to produce?"

Events: "Can we describe tangible events that would indicate that the vision had been achieved?"

By addressing these kinds of questions, we can clarify how our desired future reality will operate at multiple levels and create a more robust picture of what we want.

In our healthcare example, the mental models we might have are that we are responsible for our own health, the human body needs to be approached holistically, and prevention is the highest leverage point. Systemic structures that are consistent with those beliefs might be smaller, more individualized service providers, self-help prevention programs, and networked information systems that contain fully integrated health profiles for each person. The patterns we might hope to see are a steady decrease in preventable diseases and less reliance on symptomatic treatments. At the level of events, we would envision patients interacting with doctors in two-way conversations that are mutually respectful of each other's role and responsibility for the patient's health.

Begin describing Current Reality at the level of Events. When we move to describing current reality, we want to start at the level of events because it is usually fairly easy to rattle off "daily crises" that characterizes the current system. We can then move up through the other levels.

In healthcare, the current system can be described as one where patients sit passively while the expert "treats" them. People are bounced from one physician to the next as each specialist tries to diagnose a singular or localized cause for an ailment. These events are characterized by a pattern of behavior that has shifted the burden of wellness from the patient to the medical expert. The predominant structures that support and produce these behaviors are the doctor-patient relationships, the narrow specialties, large hospitals that treat symptoms instead of people, and a system that has no direct feedback connection between the customer, the supplier, and the payer. These structures are the manifestations of a worldview that sees the human body as a collection of parts that are to be treated when they "break down."

Articulate the operating (tacit) Vision in Current Reality. Although there may never have been an explicit vision, there is usually a tacit vision that is guiding the current reality. That is, when we look at the mental models, structures, patterns, and events, it appears as if they are being guided by an implicit vision of the way things ought to be. In healthcare, for example, the industry acts as if guided by a vision of being a disease-treatment system, where the emphasis is on efficient diagnosis and treatment of health breakdowns.

Identify Gaps or Challenges at each level. After filling in each cell under Desired Future Reality and Current Reality, we want to highlight the gaps or challenges that surface at each level.

Formulate Action Steps to close the Gaps. For each of the gaps identified, formulate the actions that will begin addressing them at each level.

Establish Indicators of Progress. In any change effort, we need ways to measure our progress. We want to be able to answer the question, "How will we know when we have arrived?" It may also be helpful to establish appropriate time frames in which to expect progress at each of the levels.

Continual and iterative process. Although the steps outlined above have been presented in a linear fashion, the vision deployment process is a continual and iterative process. The emphasis should not be so much on whether we have the matrix filled in "just right," but rather on the diligence with which we are focusing our efforts to continually clarify what goes in every part of the matrix.

Where Is the Leverage?

Our ability to influence the future increases as we move from the level of events to vision. This does not, however, mean that high-leverage actions can be found only at the higher levels. Leverage is a relative concept, not an absolute. When someone is bleeding, the highest *leverage* action at that moment is to stop the bleeding, not to formulate a vision of that person being completely healed. As we shift from looking at events to looking at shared vision, however, the focus moves from being present-oriented to being future-oriented. Consequently, the actions we take at the higher levels have more impact on *future* outcomes than on present events. (See "Summary of Action Modes" for an explanation of the types of actions that are characteristic of each level.)

In addition, our understanding of a situation at one level can feed back and inform our awareness at another level. Events and patterns of events, for example, can cause us to change systemic structures and challenge our vision. The key to successful large-scale change is to operate at all levels simultaneously as much as possible.

The Implementation Challenge:
From Vision to Reality

Articulating a compelling vision and building commitment around it marks the beginning of the journey, not the end. The greater challenge that lies ahead is to actualize the vision in every aspect of organizational life. There needs to be a clear and coherent strategy for making the vision a reality at multiple levels of the organization, including all divisions, departments, and teams. The bottom line is that in order for this work to be effective, it must be done *by individuals at each level of the organization*.

Top management may begin the deployment process by using the Vision Deployment Matrix to articulate a vision for the organization, but they also need to take the next step and invite those at the operating divisions to articulate what the vision means to them. Those managers, in turn, must invite those at the departmental level to articulate what the vision means to them, and so on (see "Organizational Deployment: An Action Plan" on p. 92).

Ultimately, visions must be real and meaningful to all those involved in order for them to be compelling and successful in transforming an organization. Although the vision deployment process may appear intensive and arduous, it is the shortest path to building an enduring shared vision.

SUMMARY OF ACTION MODES

Each level of perspective has a characteristic mode of action associated with it. To illustrate the typical actions at each level, let's use the example of a manufacturing plant that is producing defective parts:

Events. Operating at the level of events means that whenever we encounter a defective part, we sort it out and either rework it or put it on the scrap pile. We may try to correct the situation by adjusting the machinery or by inspecting more closely, but our primary mode of action is reactive.

Patterns. If we look at events (scrap rates) over a period of time, we may notice a pattern, such as higher scrap rates at certain times of the day or higher variability on some machines. We can then adapt our processes to improve the current system.

Systemic Structures. The structure of our systems is what produces the patterns and events that create our day-to-day reality. It is also where mental models and vision are translated into action. When a system is in statistical control, it means that improvement can come about only by changing the system. By working at the systemic structure level, we can create new events and patterns by altering the system, rather than just adjusting or reacting to it.

Mental Models. Where do the systemic structures come from? They are usually a product of our "mental models"—our internal pictures of how the world works. Operating at the level of mental models means understanding what our assumptions are, reflecting on them to test their relevancy, and changing them if necessary. Changing our systemic structures often requires a change in our mental images of what those structures can or ought to be.

If we can conceive of manufacturing only as one massive assembly operation, for example, then we will not be able to consider alternatives such as smaller independent manufacturing cells that can produce a higher mix of different products at lower volumes.

Vision. Surfacing, reflecting on, and changing our mental models is often a difficult and painful process. Why would we choose to go through such a process? Because we have a compelling vision of a new and different world that we are committed to creating. At the level of vision, our actions can be *generative,* bringing something into being that did not exist before. For example, a vision of providing the most options for the customer or a higher quality of work life for employees may create the impetus to reexamine old mental models of what a manufacturing plant "should" be.

Level of Perspective		Action Mode	
↑	Vision	*Generative*	Unlimited possibilities inspired by imagination and a sense of purpose.
Increasing Leverage	Mental Models	*Reflective*	Beliefs and assumptions that are congruent with the vision that we hold.
	Systemic Structures	*Creative*	Structures that are consistent with our mental models of the world.
	Patterns	*Adaptive*	Patterns of behavior that are produced by the structures.
	Events	*Reactive*	Specific events that illustrate the vision in action.

As many failed attempts at mandating visions from the top have shown, there are no short-cuts to building true shared vision. Simply put, no one can demand commitment from someone else. It is a personal choice that, once made, can be a powerful catalyst for change. ⌐

ORGANIZATIONAL DEPLOYMENT: AN ACTION PLAN

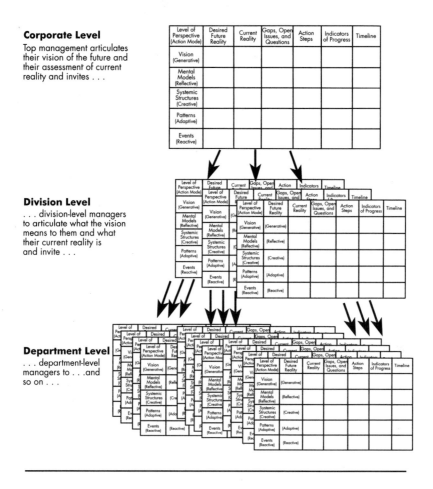

Corporate Level

Top management articulates their vision of the future and their assessment of current reality and invites . . .

Division Level

. . . division-level managers to articulate what the vision means to them and what their current reality is and invite . . .

Department Level

. . . department-level managers to . . .and so on . . .

~

Chapter Nine

From Event Thinking
to Systems Thinking

Your division has been plagued by late launches in its last five new products, and now management has charged you with "getting to the bottom of the problem." You schedule a series of management-team meetings with the goal of uncovering the source of the delays and redesigning the launch process to create on-time product releases.

The first meeting begins with a "post mortem" on the latest launch crisis. The team members tackle the issue with enthusiasm, jumping in with their own perspectives on what went wrong and why. At first the meeting seems to be going well, since everyone is obviously engaged in solving the problem. But as the meeting progresses, you start to feel like the group is spinning its wheels. The stories begin to resemble a jumble of personal anecdotes that share no common elements: "Well, on project X, we tried doing something new, and this is what happened . . ." or "This reminds me of the time when we implemented process Y and we were carrying spare parts in brown paper bags. . . ." Lots of interesting stories are being exchanged, but they do not seem to be leading to a common understanding of the problem's root causes.

The Storytelling Trap

Stories can be a powerful tool for engaging a group's interest in a problem or issue. The specific details about people and events make it easy for most people to relate to stories, and such accounts often provide a firm grounding in the day-to-day reality of the situation. But storytelling's strength is also its Achilles' heel: When we remain at event-level storytelling, it is difficult to generalize the insights to other situations, and so the solutions are often situation-specific. Without a deeper understanding of why something happened, the most we can do is find ways to react faster to similar events in the future.

Storytelling at Multiple Levels

One way that managers can move beyond event-level storytelling to a deeper understanding of an issue is to use a modified version of the Vision Deployment Matrix (see "Vision Deployment Matrix: A Framework for Large-Scale Change," p. 85). In particular, applying the first two columns of the matrix ("Current Reality" and "Desired Future Reality") to a particular problem can provide a framework for both analyzing the current situation and designing an effective, long-term solution (see "From Events to Vision: Structured Problem-Solving").

The matrix distinguishes between different levels of seeing and understanding a situation. The "Events" level captures stories about spe-

---

FROM EVENTS TO VISION: STRUCTURED PROBLEM-SOLVING

Increasing Leverage ↑

Levels of Perspective	Current Reality	Desired Future Reality
Vision	What is the current vision-in-use?	What is the espoused vision of the future?
Mental Models	What are the prevailing assumptions, beliefs, and values that sustain the systemic structures?	What assumptions, beliefs, and values are needed to realize the vision?
Systemic Structures	Which systemic structures are producing the most dominant pattern of behavior in the current system?	What kinds of systemic structures (either invented or redesigned) are required to operationalize the new mental models and achieve the vision?
Patterns	What is the behavior over time of key indicators in the current system?	What are some key indicators whose pattern of behavior shows that the desired vision is a reality?
Events	What are some specific events that characterize the current reality?	What are some specific events that illustrate how the vision is operating on a day-to-day basis?

By using a modified version of the "Vision Deployment Matrix," a team can look at a particular problem under study from different perspectives. The "Current Reality" and "Desired Future Reality" columns allow you to differentiate between diagnosis of the current situation and proposed solutions for the future.

---

cific incidents or events that indicate a problem. The next level, "Patterns," expands the time horizon. At this stage, the team might ask, "Are these individual events or stories part of a larger pattern that has been unfolding over time?" Next, the "Systemic Structures" level looks at the structures that might be producing the observed pattern of behavior. Since those systemic structures are usually physical manifestations of deeply held mental models in the organization, the "Mental Models" level prompts the team to surface them. Finally, at the "Vision" level, the group considers how the vision of what the organization is creating might be influencing those mental models.

Analyzing a problem or situation from multiple levels can be useful in several ways. First, it forces us to go beyond event-level storytelling, where our ability to affect the future is low, to a perspective that offers greater leverage for creating systemic change. Second, the matrix provides a way to distinguish between different ideas and experiences (e.g., "Does this story illustrate a problem situation or a prevalent mental model?"). Finally, when the conversation does jump from events to specific systems to assumptions and so on, the matrix can provide a coherent framework for mapping everyone's contribution in real time.

Using the Matrix

By filling in the matrix around a particular problem or issue, the team members can work together to raise their understanding from the level of events to patterns, systemic structures, mental models, and vision. For example, in the product-launch situation, the team started with stories of a particular launch failure. After some discussion, the team discovered that the proper tests for verification were never conducted. But instead of going further into the details of why that process was neglected, the team can ask questions designed to draw the stories up to the patterns level, such as, "Was this indicative of a pattern that happens on all products?" Additional stories can then be used to establish whether that is indeed a pattern.

The next step is to identify the underlying structures that may currently be responsible for such behavior. In this example, the test and verification efforts all relied on a central group of people who were chronically overloaded by all the products under development. Hence verifications were rarely done to the level specified. When the group tried to understand how engineers could justify skipping such an important step, they revealed an implicit mental model: "Not knowing there is a problem and moving forward is better than knowing there is a problem and moving forward." In short, the division had been operating according to an "ignorance is bliss" strategy.

To understand where this assumption came from, the group asked, "What is the implicit vision driving the process?" The most common answer was "to minimize unwanted senior management attention." In other words, no one in product development wanted to have problems surface on their "watch."

Although this team focused on the "Current Reality" column, they could also fill out the "Desired Future Reality" column by asking what kinds of new structures might be needed to prevent these problems from happening in the future.

Guiding Questions

The following set of questions can be used to guide conversations as a team moves among the different levels of perspective. In looking at current reality, it may be easier to start at the level of events (since that is where stories usually begin) and work your way up the levels. When mapping out the desired future reality, however, it may be better to begin at the level of vision and go down to the other levels so that your desired future reality is not limited by the current reality. Having said that, it is likely that in actual meetings the conversation will bounce all over the place. The main point is to use the matrix to capture the conversation in a coherent framework.

Current Reality

- What are some specific events that characterize the current reality?
- Are those specific events indicative of a pattern over time? Do other stories corroborate this repeated pattern?
- Are there systemic structures in place that are responsible for the pattern? Which specific structures are producing the most dominant pattern of behavior behind the current results?
- What mental models do we hold that led us to put such structures in place? What are the prevailing assumptions, beliefs, and values that sustain those structures?

- What kind of vision are we operating out of that explains the mental models we hold? What is the current vision-in-use?

Desired Future Reality

- What is the espoused vision of the future?
- What sets of assumptions, beliefs, and values will help realize the vision?
- What kinds of systemic structures are required (either invented or redesigned) to operationalize the new mental models and achieve that vision?
- What would be the behavior over time of key indicators if the desired vision became a reality?
- What specific events would illustrate how the vision is operating on a day-to-day basis?

By elevating the conversation from events to systems structure and beyond, this simple tool can help managers make clearer sense of their own experiences, and use those experiences to formulate more effective solutions to the problems at hand. ⌐

≋

Chapter Ten

Levels of Perspective: "Firefighting" at Multiple Levels

I t's another busy night in the hospital emergency room. Several car-accident victims have been rushed into surgery, one little boy is having a broken arm set, a drug overdose victim is being treated, and numerous other people fill the chairs in the waiting room. Each night is different, and yet they are all the same. The doctors and nurses must act fast to treat the most seriously injured, while the others wait their turn. Like an assembly line of defective parts, patients are diagnosed, treated, and then released. Each injury is a crisis that demands immediate attention.

So what's wrong with this picture? After all, isn't this what emergency rooms are meant to do? The answer depends on the level of perspective at which we are looking at the situation.

Levels of Perspective

There are multiple levels from which we can view and perceive the world. From a systemic perspective, we are interested in five distinct levels—events, patterns of behavior, systemic structures, mental models, and vision (see "Levels of Perspective" on p. 100).

- *Events* are the things we encounter on a day-to-day basis: A machine breaks; it rains; we eat dinner, see a movie, or write a report. This is the level of most people's direct experience of the world.
- *Patterns of Behavior over Time* are the accumulation of events which, when strung together as a series, can reveal recurring patterns over

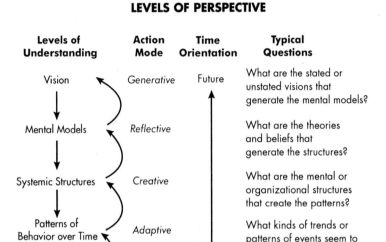

LEVELS OF PERSPECTIVE

Levels of Understanding	Action Mode	Time Orientation	Typical Questions
Vision	Generative	Future	What are the stated or unstated visions that generate the mental models?
Mental Models	Reflective		What are the theories and beliefs that generate the structures?
Systemic Structures	Creative		What are the mental or organizational structures that create the patterns?
Patterns of Behavior over Time	Adaptive		What kinds of trends or patterns of events seem to be recurring?
Events	Reactive	Present	What is the fastest way to react to this event NOW?

time. These patterns serve as "systemic structure detectors" in that, if you identify a pattern, systemic structures are likely responsible for producing those patterns.

- *Systemic Structures* refer to the systems, structures, processes, policies, and procedures that are part of an organization's infrastructures for making its operations run. In turn, these structures can be viewed as "pattern generators" because they are responsible for producing the events that form a recognizable pattern.

- *Mental Models*, our deepest beliefs and theories about the world, can be viewed as the "systemic structure generators" because they are like the guiding specifications responsible for creating structures.

- *Vision* can be viewed as the guiding image that "sponsors" all of our mental models.

All five levels are important for developing a systems thinking perspective, especially because we live in an event-oriented world, and our language is often rooted in that level. At work, we encounter a series of events, which often appear in the form of problems that we must "solve." Our solutions, however, may be short-lived, and the symptoms can eventually return as seemingly new problems.

Multiple Action Modes for Leverage

When things happen at the events level, they usually require an immediate response. This is consistent with our evolutionary history, which was geared toward responding to sudden events—those things that pose an immediate danger to our well-being. That capability may have been all we needed to survive when we lived in small tribes as hunter-gatherers. But, in our modern world of complex social systems, the greatest threats to our survival or health are often far less obvious or immediate, though no less deadly. This is why we need to expand our repertoire of actions beyond the reactive, to understand what it means to take adaptive, creative, reflective, and generative actions.

Reactive. If a house is burning, for example, the highest leverage action we can take in the moment is to be reactive and put out the fire. In other words, that is not the best time to stop and conduct a family meeting to gain consensus on what is the best course of action! Or, if you find yourself in front of a runaway bus, that is not the time to become reflective and wonder about how you could have prevented such a situation from happening. In both cases, reactive actions provide the highest leverage. However, if all we ever do is react, then we are forever doomed to keep reacting.

Adaptive. Taking adaptive actions at the patterns level provides us with a different level of leverage. As firefighters, for example, we can begin to anticipate where fires are more likely to occur by noticing that certain neighborhoods seem to have more fires than others. We can then adapt to this pattern by locating more fire stations in those areas, and staffing them accordingly (based on past patterns of usage). Because the stations are a lot closer, we can be more effective at putting out fires by getting to them sooner. Being adaptive allows us to anticipate and be prepared, and therefore, can be less disruptive than simply being reactive. But still, at this level, our actions are mostly reactive actions disguised as proactive (essentially, pre-emptive reactive actions!).

Creative. At the systemic structure level, we begin asking questions like: "Are smoke detectors being used? What kinds of building materials are less flammable? What safety features reduce fatalities?" Actions taken at this level can actually reduce the number and severity of fires. Establishing fire codes with requirements such as automatic sprinkler systems, fireproof materials, fire walls, and fire-alarm systems saves lives by preventing or containing fires. Actions taken at this level are creative because they help create different patterns and events.

Reflective. Where do systemic structures come from? They are created based on our mental models about the kinds of structures we believe will best serve our needs. The structures reflect our deep-rooted beliefs about what we consider to be the best or "right" way to do things. These beliefs are the ones that provide continual support for the existing systemic structures to stay in place. If we are to be effective at this level, we must take more reflective actions—ones that help us surface, suspend, and test our own (and others') mental models. Notice that the word "change" is not in that list. This is because the minute we start taking actions to change somebody's mental models, we lose the leverage of taking reflective actions and fall back into taking reactive actions—with predictable results.

Generative. At the level of vision, we hold an image in our minds (consciously or unconsciously) that guides what we do on a day-to-day basis. In the case of firefighting, new mental models (e.g., a shift in forestry from preventing fires to starting pre-emptive fires) were born out of a shift in vision from simply stopping the immediate dangers of forest fires to creating a healthy ecosystem over the long term. At the level of vision, we begin to take generative actions by asking questions like "What's the purpose of fighting forest fires in the first place? What is it that we truly care about creating?"

Our ability to influence the future increases as we move from the level of events to vision. Does this mean that high-leverage actions can only be found at the higher levels? No. Leverage is a relative concept, not an absolute. When someone is bleeding, the highest leverage action at that moment is to stop the bleeding. Any other action would be inappropriate. As we move up the levels from events to vision, however, the focus moves from being present-oriented to being future-oriented. Consequently, the actions we take at the higher levels have more impact on future outcomes, and less on current events.

Moving from a Reactive to a Generative Orientation

In conducting many workshops with managers over the years, I have asked them to conduct their own diagnosis about the action mode that drives most of their actions. The results come back consistently that 80 to 90 percent of their actions tend to be reactive or adaptive. That's both bad news and good news. The bad news is the high percentage of reactive/adaptive actions. So what's the good news? Well, if people had diagnosed that they were actually taking the appropriate high-leverage action at each level and still were not getting the results they wanted, that would be bad news indeed!

One of the most important messages of the "Levels of Perspective" framework is that we must recognize the level at which we are operating, and evaluate whether taking the corresponding action provides the highest leverage for that situation. Each level offers different opportunities for high-leverage action, but they also have their limits. The challenge is to choose the appropriate response for the immediate situation and find ways to change the future by operating at multiple levels in multiple action modes.

It is also important to remember that the process of gaining deeper understanding is not a linear one (from events to vision). Our understanding of a situation at one level can feed back and inform our awareness at another level. Events and patterns, for example, can cause us to change systemic structures and can also challenge our mental models. To be most effective, we must consider the full range of levels carefully and we must resist the tendency to work at only one or two levels to the exclusion of the others. ⤳

Index
to The Systems Thinker™
Newsletter

From Fragmentation to Integration: Building Learning Communities
(V8N4, May 1997)

Managing Organizational Learning Cycles
(V3N8, October 1992)

Leveraging Competence to Build Organizational Capability
(V9N1, February 1998)

Building Learning Infrastructures
(V5N3, April 1994)

Paradigm-Creating Loops: How Perceptions Shape Reality
(V4N2, March 1993)

TQM and Systems Thinking as Theory-Building Tools
(V5N2, March 1994)

What Is Your Organization's Core Theory of Success?
(V8N3, April 1997)

From Key Success Factors to Key Success Loops
(V8N5, June/July 1997)

Vision Deployment Matrix: A Framework for Large-Scale Change
(V6N1, February 1995)

From Event Thinking to Systems Thinking
(V7N4, May 1996)

Levels of Understanding: "Firefighting" at Multiple Levels
(V4N5, June/July, 1993)